Until Each One Has a Home

Heartfelt Stories from DunRoamin' Stray and Rescue, a Canadian Pet Rescue

Mildred A. Drost DVM

Until Each One Has a Home
Copyright © 2016 by Mildred A. Drost DVM

No part of this publication may be reproduced, distributed, or transmitted in any form or by any means, including photocopying, recording, or other electronic or mechanical methods, without the prior written permission of the author, except in the case of brief quotations embodied in critical reviews and certain other non-commercial uses permitted by copyright law.

tellwell

Tellwell Talent
www.tellwell.ca

ISBN
978-1-77302-169-0 (Paperback)
978-1-77302-168-3 (eBook)

All of God's creatures have a place in the choir.

Bill Staines

This book is dedicated to those who advocate for and protect animals—for their selflessness and caring

Table of Contents

INTRODUCTION xiii
LESTER 1
SAVING LIVES CAN START WITH YOU 4
RAINING KITTENS 7
UNCHAIN MY HEART 10
FOSTERING 12
THANK YOU FOR YOUR DONATION 16
RAINBOW BRIDGE 20
YOU MAY THROW AWAY A LIFESAVER 22
CUTEST PUPPY 24
'TWAS THE NIGHT BEFORE CHRISTMAS 27
BENTON REGINALD SEYMOUR BLACK 30
UNWANTED PETS 33
"THEY'RE OKAY NOW!" 36
ROGUE 38
ABANDONED KITTENS - DON'T LITTER 41
HOW MANY BLOWS IS "UNDUE"? 43

BONES	45
DO YOU KNOW WHERE YOUR PET IS?	48
LITTLE JOE HENRI	51
DUNBREEDIN'	54
STRAY THOUGHTS	56
NOT A TIME TO KILL	58
HOGAN	61
TATER TOTS	64
ALL DOGS GO TO HEAVEN	66
THE DUNROAMIN' VET'S CHRISTMAS	69
THANKS	71
FIGHT TERRIERISM	74
FREE DOG	76
THE DOG WHO CAME IN FROM THE COLD	78
BORN TO LOSE	80
ROMEOW	82
DIXON	85
LOUP	88
MAN'S BEST FRIENDS	91
THE BEATLES AT DUNROAMIN'	93
AVA	96
THE PAIN OF CHAINS	98
LANDON	101
TAKING A BITE OUT OF LIFE	104
KITTENS, KITTENS, KITTENS	107
BABY MIKEY	110
OAKLEY	113
WHO'S HUGH?	116
LESSONS WE HAVE LEARNED FROM OUR STRAYS	119
LET'S ALL BE DUNROAMIN'	123

LINK	126
TEACH THEM!	129
FERAL AT DUNROAMIN'	132
I AM A DUNROAMIN' VOLUNTEER	135
CHRISTMAS	138
PUPPY FARM CHRISTMAS	140
DAILY REPORT	143
IS "GOOD ENOUGH" THEN "GOOD ENOUGH" NOW?	146
HILTON	149
FREEMAN & ME	151
DREYFUS	155
SO I HERD!	158
WHO, IF NOT YOU?	161
A DUNROAMIN' SITUATION	164
IKE	168
ITCHY	170
WHY DO WE DO THIS?	172
ROYALTY	175
DYING FOR ATTENTION	178
GULLIVER	180
THEY SURE CAN MULTIPLY	183
BRINGING HOME THE STANLEY PUP	186
PET OVERPOPULATION	190
OVERSTOCK SALE!	192
PRICELESS DOGS	194
SPAY IT FORWARD	197
JUST THERE	200
KITTIES ARE SO NICE	202
NOBLESS OBLIGE	205
STANDARDS	208

DISENCHANTMENT RANT	210
PURRCEPTION	213
DUNROAMIN' TELEPHONE LOG, SEPTEMBER 2011	216
IKAT BEATS AN APPLE EVERY TIME	219
ROGER	222
WE'RE RESPONSIBLE!	224
IN THE DUNROAMIN' NEWS	227
CHRISTMAS POEM	230
HEAT	232
TEACH YOUR CHILDREN (TWO- OR FOUR-LEGGED)	235
PET LOSS	239
MAKE IT ALL WELL FOR YOUR DOG	242
RANDALL	245
WORLD SPAY DAY	248
THE QUEEN OF SPAYEDS	250
SEVEN	252
YOUR DONATIONS AT WORK	254
YOU GOTTA CARE	257
PRESS 1	261
JERRY	265
THINGS	268
GOODBYE IKE	272
IT'S ALL ABOUT THE ANIMALS	276
THE SAD LOSS OF A WONDERFUL PET	279
ADOPTING DREYFUS	281
TOO MANY PETS	286
BERNICE	289
BOGART	292
ANNIE	294

RIP BOGART	296
MANLEY	298
I-LEAN	300
SPAY AND NEUTER	302
CLAWED?	305
DIARY OF AN UNCHAINED DOG	310
GREAT SCOT	314
MEET DUNROAMIN'S BARACK	317
THE SAINT BERNARD DOG BLOG	319
DUNROAMIN'S OMEN	327
WILEY	330
SOME OF MY FOSTER DOGS	333
HALLE PLEAS FOR HELP	338
AFTERWORD:	341

INTRODUCTION

Animal rescuing and sheltering is a turbulent, taxing and stressful labour of caring for its workers. Mostly, it is done because of a strong love of the animals and a total rejection of the amount of suffering that some animals endure. The highs of animal rescue can be extreme— as can the lows. It can seem like a bipolar disorder, soaring, grinning and celebrating a win for one particular animal one day, and the next, feeling the depths of despair for the failure to win for another, imagining the suffering endured by that individual for no justifiable reason.

It can make one ashamed to be part of the human race, just before it makes you so proud of someone that you can hardly speak. You see the best and the worst of society and along with that, you see what society does to, and does for, its animals.

What follows is a series of essays or articles, resulting from my responses and those of others, to specific situations encountered by DunRoamin' Stray and Rescue, Inc., over a period of several years. Some articles celebrate animals - some strays, some pets. Others rail at the abuses and neglect of companion animals seen in our rural area of New Brunswick, Canada.

DunRoamin' evolved from attempts to assist and relieve suffering of the stray animals brought to my veterinary clinic by concerned individuals who had found them, injured or sick and needing veterinary care, but with no owner to pay for treatment. Gradually, clients of the clinic became aware of our sideline and started to contribute to costs of medications and surgeries required by these stray animals. Others offered to foster the recovering animals until they were healthy, most of the original strays being adopted by clinic staff or clients.

As word spread about our sideline, more and more strays were brought for help. Donations also increased, until we felt that records and accountability were necessary. This endeavour needed a name. Since our dogs and cats were all done roaming when they came to us, we decided that DunRoamin' was a fitting name for our rescue.

This rescue, which specializes in injured and sick unowned animals that would be too much for the existing shelter system to manage, both physically and financially, has grown to be an entity to be reckoned with and has taken on the task of educating the public on animal care as well as advocating for all animals.

As part of our attempts to reach out to the communities and to help change attitudes towards and increase respect for our animals, I began to write weekly articles which were published in our local newspaper, The Bugle-Observer, in Woodstock, NB. The articles appeared under the title "We're All DunRoamin'"

The intent was to make people aware of the difficulties encountered by these pets, the issues surrounding abandonment, abuse and neglect and to try to sponsor a feeling of compassion and concern for the welfare of homeless or abused animals. We felt strongly that if people were aware of the extent of the abuse, neglect and abandonment, they would be impacted in a positive way, working to reduce it and taking responsibility for their own pets. We stressed that the first step in reducing this problem was to spay and neuter pets, repeating, over and over, that allowing pets to reproduce in a climate where animals were already thrown away like garbage, was not in the interests of the discarded animals or the newly minted ones, many of which would also be discarded.

Another task was to make people see that these animals felt the same pain - physical and emotional, that we would feel in a similar situation. They felt fear, loneliness, depression and anxiety. Surprisingly, I knew from discussions with some clients that we needed to point out that animals also felt cold, thirst, hunger, pain and heat the same way we do (although their ways of showing these discomforts were different from ours, but evident to the trained eye).

So, prompted by haunting recent events - or perhaps a quirky, misplaced thought or two, these articles were the result of my involvement with the "incoming" at DunRoamin' Stray and Rescue, Inc. Some were meant to be funny and entertaining with an underlying message. Others were meant to be blunt, accusatory or despairing, with a glaring message. All were meant to give a voice to animals, both strays and pets, and to celebrate their uniqueness, their goodness and their value as living beings. Christmas enthusiasts will, no doubt, recognise the inclusion and mutilation of several iconic Yuletide poems and songs. These have been included as they were such fun to write and were meant to lighten the mood.

Although these articles were written about events that affected DunRoamin' Stray and Rescue, in New Brunswick, Canada, they could well have been written about events in most rescues and animal shelters, whether in Canada, the US or other countries. These incidents and attitudes are not specific to our region. They are specific to our species. While legions of animal advocates struggle to protect these sentient creatures, it seems that equal numbers seek to inflict harm and suffering on them. Animals' lives and comfort are every bit as important to them as ours are to us. We need to know that and accept them as valuable, sentient beings.

Maybe this book can help some people to see our animal friends in a new light, and to treat them with the understanding and compassion that they deserve. Maybe people will recognize the need to take responsibility for their part in the suffering, if they are allowing their pets to breed. Maybe people will decide to spare the world more unwanted animals by making lifetime commitments to their pets and by spaying and neutering their animals.

LESTER

He came through the door in a flurry of movement – white teeth flashing in a wide grin, brown eyes sparkling with mischief, jet black hair shining in the morning sun. He moved with a loose-limbed, barely restrained gait. His eyes met mine and I felt like the most important person in the room. He was interested in everything about me – where I'd been, who I knew, how I lived. His interest held no bounds, and it seemed like forever before he had enough information from me. He was acutely interested in the smallest details. As I got to know him better, I became aware of his total goodness, his complete lack of antipathy, his unparalleled capacity for love.

I thought to myself, *"Darn! I'm in love again!"* And I was. He made me laugh, made me smile, made me feel important, interesting and safe. He brightened my life and made me notice the little things again – a butterfly, a hummingbird, a grasshopper. Nothing was too small or too mundane to escape his notice. He lived his life to the fullest, enjoying every day, revelling in the simple pleasures of life— a good meal, a quick hug, a wet kiss, a companionable walk. Okay, I admit that, with scarcely a second thought, I let Lester move in with me. Who wouldn't? I was smitten!

With unbridled enthusiasm, Lester moved into my house and it has not been the same since. The floors seem cleaner and brighter. Meals take on a new importance. Walks are more interesting. The house is neater, the quiet more appreciated and profound. I notice the little things and find new pleasure in them.

No, he's not housetrained, but he's working on it. He's not leash-trained, but he's learning. He's not kennel trained, but he hardly said a word in his crate last night, and he only jumped up on me twice yesterday. That's not bad for a five-month old pup!

Three days. Just three. That's all the time he had from the moment he was picked up as a stray. The law allows him three days – seventy-two hours! If no one claims him in seventy-two hours, he can be killed. That's because he is disposable in our society – of no value, useless. It is of no interest that he is a mere baby, one who is all goodness, who has barely started to live. Three days – that's all he gets. Thankfully, the Animal Control Officer recognized the goodness in this pup and, unable to place him in a shelter, asked DunRoamin' to take him in.

So - "He's okay now", – as we say! We'll find a home for him no matter how long it takes. But the obscenity of this whole situation, the overpopulation of pet animals, the breeding of pets in an overpopulated world, the discarding or killing of beautiful healthy pups who are all goodness – it's heartbreaking! It's the little guys like Lester who pay the price for our own laziness, our refusal to control the breeding of our pets.

What does it say about our world when all that goodness— all that love— is worth nothing?

With these laws and this attitude, animals are put down all the time. But, think about this – in this area where we live, a rural agricultural area, the numbers of stray animals who could be killed due to overfilled shelters is appalling. So, we help as much as we can.

We know it's not nameless, faceless, unknown dogs and cats who could be killed because of indiscriminate breeding of and homelessness of our pets. Look at our website! It's Lester, Midas and Leland, Goliath, Ester and Purrcy, Henri, Ferris, and Ashton, Mariah, Clover and Diva, Piper, Harvey and Spike, Willis, Sage and William, Dharma, Gritty and Grime...

SAVING LIVES CAN START WITH YOU

People ask me, "How can I get rid of the smelly old cat with all the sores that is hanging around my house?" They say, "I've chased him away, I've thrown water on him, I've done everything that I can think of but he's still hanging around!"

My first thought is *"Does he need help? Is he injured? Is he asking you to help him?"*

I ask them, "Can you help him? Bring him in out of the cold and feed him? Can you keep him warm and safe and fed until we can find a safe place for him to stay? Can you have his injuries treated?"

Often, after a few moments of thought, the answer is "Yes, I can! I didn't think about bringing him in because he looks so bad!" And yet, that is precisely why you should help.

What if, after you chased him away from your front step and doused him with water, he died there in your yard, of cold, starvation and infection— after he had asked you for help?

Too often we see these poor cats, raised in the comfort of a home and then abandoned near a barn because *there are lots of mice in the barn*. But, who will teach the Whiskas-fed cat to hunt? Who will show them who the predators are and how to escape them? Who will show them where to find warmth in this open, unheated barn? Where will they find water?

We see these cats - their bony, starved little bodies shivering with cold, skin torn by predator attacks or attacks by other cats, infected eyes wide with confusion and fear. They are often just hours or days from dying of infection, starvation and injury. We treat their wounds, re-hydrate them, place them in warm, comfortable, safe surroundings and serve them food and water. The cat struggles to eat and drink, using his jaw as a shovel to put the life-saving nutrition and fluid into his emaciated body. We feed them small meals, hourly until they finally seem satiated. We settle them and assure them that they are now safe. Then, the purring begins, the feet start to knead and the cat starts to relax in the first safe refuge that he has seen since his abandonment. His eyes soften, and, blissfully, the cat falls asleep, safe at last.

He sleeps and eats for 2 weeks, awakening for short periods, so he can purr for his rescuers and caretakers. He begins the long process of grooming himself and healing. Two weeks later, each hair arranged with perfect precision, bones covered with light padding, sleep deprivation resolved, he begins to play.

His caretakers huddle around him, grinning delightedly. Word spreads. HE'S PLAYING!

Debt? Paid in full.

RAINING KITTENS

In the last month DunRoamin' has received thirty-one, one-month old kittens. We are in crisis mode now, trying to triage the sickest to be admitted to the clinic and decide which could be sent to foster homes for care. They are so fragile, these little ones, obviously having had a very poor start in life! DunRoamin' is struggling to give proper care to these poor little mites and we are determined to do our best. Our volunteers are coming to the rescue.

DunRoamin' was established to help those animals who fell through the cracks of the existing shelter system. This includes:

- those too sick to go to shelters;
- those with fractures and illnesses that shelters cannot afford to treat
- those severely starved due to abandonment or neglect

- those physically abused and too frightened to be handled, and those too young to be exposed to the diseases that may be brought to a shelter.

We also try to educate people to improve the care and management of pets.

DunRoamin' is not a dumping ground for unwanted cats and kittens. The other day a gentleman walked in with a cardboard box full of kittens. "I have kittens for you," he cheerily said. It turns out these were the offspring of his two house cats which he had taken in last fall. "Well, I can't keep them," he said. "I already have two cats! I'll have to do away with them then. I'll have to drown them in the mop pail!" He is not the only one with this attitude. Several cats and kittens have been abandoned on the doorstep of the Clinic over the past couple of weeks. Neither DunRoamin' nor the Florenceville Veterinary Clinic is a shelter. We try to help animals in dire straits. We do this on our own time, with our own funds and those donated and raised for us by our supporters. We take responsibility for abandoned kittens, injured cats and dogs, those who are homeless, and we try to help any animal that is within our power to help.

It is irresponsible and contrary to the Society for the Prevention of Cruelty to Animals (SPCA) Act to abandon animals or to kill them (by drowning, as is often threatened). Those acts are acts of cruelty and can be punishable under the Criminal Code of Canada.

With the abundance of animals needing to find homes, volunteers and shelters are desperately trying to feed, house and care for these poor souls. There is no good reason for your family pet to be adding to the problem. A simple operation before six months of age will prevent kitten and pup abandonment, suffering and the forced killing of unwanted pets in shelters.

Most shelters cannot deal with the sheer numbers of strays and drop-offs that are arriving. If your pet is reproducing, you are responsible for their offspring. Be responsible and have your pets spayed and neutered. Help your local shelter by not producing any more animals that have nowhere to go!

UNCHAIN MY HEART

Do you still tie your dog outside day and night, day after day, winter and summer? Don't you ever let him loose for exercise or bring him into the house for companionship and friendly interaction? Don't you see how severely that limits his life? Don't you see how it stops him from being with you, his pack? Don't you see how it stops him from learning and developing into a well-rounded, well-socialized pet? Don't you see how it blocks his potential? Don't you see that he is nothing but a chained prisoner? He can't even guard his family! It creates boredom and frustration. It forces him to live in his own excrement. It causes neuroses and hostility. It causes aggression. It prevents him from running and playing. It stops him from being a dog. It makes him a captive!

Life on a chain is worse than no life at all. And do you know the most heartbreaking part of it all? If you went out there and released him right now, after all this time, he'd still be so happy to see you, so excited to be with you, so gratified for the chance to be your dog, to be close to you and live with you, that he'd forgive you in a heartbeat - because he is a dog and because you set him free to be one.

Why not try a little experiment? Go out into your yard and stand there until I call you. I'll put a chain around your leg to simulate your dog's experience. Then wait, while the minutes tick endlessly by. Maybe you'll wait for a half hour. Maybe I'll forget to call you. Then record how you feel. Bored? Frustrated? Irritated? Restless? Angry? Helpless? Lonely? Confused? Frightened? Depressed? Isolated? Forgotten? Any positive feelings? No, huh. Think about your dog. That's his life. I'm not saying "Don't put your dog on a rope when he goes out to do his business, or if you are close to the road." I'm saying "Don't leave your dog isolated at the back of your lot. Don't make that his life." I'm saying "Bring him into the house. Let him interact with family. Take him for a walk. Play with him. Let him have a life!" If you won't do it—then please give him to someone who will!

Dogs are here to be our friends, to make us smile, to show us unconditional love, to make us laugh, to encourage us to be silly, to lower our blood pressure, to teach us to be better human beings. Dogs certainly are man's best friends. But man? Often man falls very short of being a dog's best friend. Bring your dog inside! Give him the life he deserves. Be your dog's best friend - that's all he wants.

FOSTERING

Well, we at DunRoamin' feel like we've hit the jackpot again - the cat jackpot. We know it's not literally "raining cats and dogs," but it sure seems that way. We have pleaded with everyone we know (and some that we don't know) to foster the influx of mothers, kittens and "expecting" mothers that have come from the streets and the woods. Otherwise, those expectant mothers may find they get more than was expected- I mean more cold, more malnutrition, more harassment by wildlife and people and more kitten mortality. Since we are always asking for foster families, I thought that I would explain exactly what is involved in fostering our cats, and our reasons for wanting them out in homes. These reasons vary due to age, condition and socialization of the animals.

For example, we have two groups of two healthy fourteen to sixteen week old kittens in foster care right now. They came from feral conditions and their foster families are trying to socialize them to the point where they can be adopted out to the luxurious life of a house cat. It's their best chance at a decent life. If these cats are not tameable (they have to have had some contact with people in their early weeks to become completely tame), we will be forced to place them in barns, etc. where they will be monitored, fed, and trapped for medical care. There are some farms where this situation is set up and sometimes this is all that we can offer. The life of a wild animal in captivity (i.e. caged in a shelter, or constantly living in fear of the humans in proximity) is not an option that we can promote. So, we spay or neuter, address all medical needs and vaccinate. Then we release them to the only life that they can now accept.

Another family has a litter of kittens, no mother. These kittens require observation to note that each tiny guy is thriving and gaining as it should. Doting foster parents note the frequency, quality and consistency of each kitten's excrement and monitor the activity levels and other indicators of health. Problems are reported to the DunRoamin' vets, who address these concerns. Kittens live in foster homes until they are fully vaccinated, to protect them from diseases that may be encountered at the vet hospital. They are then brought back to DunRoamin' for adoption.

Other very pregnant cats, too, are sent to foster homes to birth their kittens, safely protected from cat communicable diseases at the clinic and to reduce stress on the mother. Also, cats who cannot cope with the stress of communal living, or who just need to receive some TLC to relearn that people can be trusted are sent to foster homes. Occasionally, an injured cat may heal in a foster home, again, TLC being the best medicine.

So, I bet you are wondering, what does fostering require from me? Well, TLC, monitoring for problems, a safe, quiet environment (perhaps a spare room, a laundry room, or even a cat condo - supplied by us, or in some cases, free roam of your house), food, warmth and a commitment to keep the cats indoors. That's it! Don't even have to walk them or throw the ball for them, and they almost never chew your shoes or their beds.

DunRoamin' is prepared to supply cat condos, food, litter, toys, beds, litter boxes, and all kinds of advice. Some foster families like to be responsible for everything the cats need - we supply all the veterinary care. Others prefer to have supplies provided. DunRoamin' is fine with both - the essential items that we are short on are time to deliver TLC and provisions for individual attention.

A new mother may require up to two months of fostering, until her kittens are weaned. Then she can be spayed and we can get on with finding her a permanent residence. The kittens themselves may be twelve to fourteen weeks (ideally) before they are safe to return to the herd. Some animals require days, weeks or months of special care.

A final word if you are thinking of offering your home for fostering: to protect your own animals from possible contagious diseases that our unfortunate street cats may have acquired, we require that your own pets are vaccinated and in good health. You must agree to keep our fosters inside where they are safe and warm, and adhere to the policies as indicated on the Foster Parent's Agreement which may be seen at the veterinary clinic , or on our website www.dunroaminstrayandrescue.com.

We desperately hope that you will consider discussing the option of fostering the little guys who struggle so to survive in our world. I can think of nothing more rewarding than being involved in saving a desperate little life.

THANK YOU FOR YOUR DONATION

It is interesting to note human behaviour in regards to their expectations and response to learning that the Florenceville Veterinary Clinic, through it's connections to DunRoamin', has helped injured and sick stray animals. Some have decided that, since we like animals so much, it is okay to dump their own excess pets on our doorstep. Finding traumatized and abandoned animals on our doorstep frequently during the cold weather has caused many of our staff to comment bitterly on the disrespect shown to the animals as well as to our attempts to assist those animals with no options. It also ties up many staff members as they try to capture the scattered animals to prevent them from being hit by vehicles. One situation in particular prompted the following, which was printed in our local paper.

A short open letter to the anonymous person who left the huge donation on the steps of the Florenceville Veterinary Clinic:

To Whom It May Concern -

Thank you so much for the huge donation that we discovered on the steps of the Florenceville Veterinary Clinic the other morning. We are sorry that you were not able to come in during business hours, and perhaps we should consider being opened all night so as to accommodate your needs.

Our security cameras revealed that you were in a bit of a hurry and, had we been present, we would have happily assisted you with your boxes. Thankfully, they did not appear to be very heavy and you made quick work of getting them unloaded.

We found your name amongst the papers and tags on the empty boxes, but were unable to make out your address. We would appreciate it if you could call us with your address so that we can express our gratitude for your selfless contribution.

It is not often that we are treated to such a big surprise on arriving at work in the morning. It was the first time we'd had to search all the crevasses around the building with no knowledge of the number of cats we were searching for. (We knew we were looking for cats since your note said they were all litter trained). Hours later, our total was seven, and we pray that that was the sum total. Our staff was late in admitting our surgery patients that day and several clients were forced to wait while staff rounded up the little ones, who were in great danger from constant traffic in the area. Although clients were very understanding when informed of the cause of the delays, most were appalled at the act of abandonment.

Both mother cats are doing quite well. They have been treated for severe flea infestations and malnourishment, aggravated by their severe worm burdens. Once they reach an acceptable body weight and the kittens are weaned, we will spay them to prevent further litters.

The kittens— we found five— are improving, although it does take them longer to recover from such severe flea burdens, on top of malnutrition. Some even die from severe anemia caused by these parasites. We have also attended to their severe ear mite infestations and hope that the pain will subside soon. These kittens, too, will be vaccinated when healthy enough, and spayed and neutered as well.

The influx that morning has placed a severe strain on our budget, as we work very hard to raise our operating costs through donations and fundraisers. We hope that we will still be able to attend to the injured and sick *strays* that are brought to us (as that is our mandate) with what remains of our budget.

If you will note our sign in the future, it reads "Veterinary Clinic." Shelters are present in Debec, Arthurette, and Fredericton. Perhaps an easier resolution in the future, for all concerned, especially these poor cats, would be trying a spay/neuter option with your pets. This is your responsibility and the only way to prevent a recurrence of this situation.

Please give us a call, as we would really love to talk with you in person. Your thoughtfulness certainly made our week, and we don't know how to thank you.

Warmest regards

DunRoamin

RAINBOW BRIDGE

Over the past twenty-five years or so, I have had a relatively constant seven or eight dogs living with me at any one time - Malamutes, rescues, or strays. I've never tried to total the number of canine friends to which I have been a guardian, but assume the total would be large.

A few years ago, when I was in vet school, one of my favourite Malamutes, Timber, was diagnosed with kidney cancer, and despite all attempts to save him, he succumbed to his disease. I was given a copy of an article/story by an unknown author entitled "Rainbow Bridge" which follows. After reading this, I felt better, somehow, in my loss. I have offered this to my clients in hopes of relieving some of their sadness and lifting some of their pain under similar circumstances.

> *Just this side of heaven is a place called Rainbow Bridge. When an animal dies that has been*

especially close to someone here, that pet goes to Rainbow Bridge. There are meadows and hills for all of our special friends so they can run and play together. There is plenty of food, water and sunshine, and our friends are warm and comfortable.

All the animals who had been ill and old are restored to health and vigour. Those who were hurt or maimed are made whole and strong again, just as we remember them in our dreams of days and times gone by. The animals are happy and content, except for one small thing: they each miss someone very special to them who had to be left behind.

They all run and play together, but the day comes when one suddenly stops and looks into the distance. His bright eyes are intent. His eager body quivers. Suddenly he begins to run from the group, flying over the green grass, his legs carrying him faster and faster.

You have been spotted, and when you and your special friend finally meet, you cling together in joyous reunion, never to be parted again. The happy kisses rain upon your face; your hands again caress the beloved head, and you look once more into the trusting eyes of your pet, so long gone from your life, but never absent from your heart.

Then you cross Rainbow Bridge together.

After reading this for the first time, a friend turned to me and said, in an awed voice, "You're going to be trampled!"

YOU MAY THROW AWAY A LIFESAVER

Many of DunRoamin's animals are "throw-away" pets - that cute kitten who grew into a cat, that pup who got so big. Adopting dogs and cats is at least a fourteen-year commitment and people should take this into consideration before getting a pet. They are aware, sentient, feeling individuals. That they would be thrown away, like empty McDonald's packages or Tim Horton cups is obscene. How else would you describe the abandonment of lovely young pups thrown out in the woods, the abandonment of kittens in ditches, and so on?

Here's another angle to these stories. Howard, now, is a beautiful buff and white cat, well loved and well looked after. He was found abandoned and very sick near the water in Grand Falls, and when brought to us by his rescuer, fell deeply and permanently in love with a cat-lover friend. Not long after this "love at first sight" couple moved in together, she was having work done in her home. The workman was using a large motor-driven machine in her basement and its faulty motor let off large amounts of carbon monoxide gases. Howie's new love, resting on her sofa upstairs, drifted off to sleep, unaware of the danger. Not Howard! He leapt onto her lap and began hitting her face and nose, even using his claws and teeth to awaken her. Both stumbled outdoors into the fresh air and then entered the basement to alert the very drowsy workman. That's two lives saved! Throw-away cat.

Another of our strays, Elaine, a house cat, was abandoned along with her two young kittens when her family moved away. After struggling for weeks to survive and to feed and protect her young, she was found and became a DunRoamin' cat. She was then gratefully adopted by a lady whose daughter was very ill. Elaine became best of friends with the young woman who suffered episodes which were life-threatening. Soon, the mother noted Elaine running to her from her daughter's room, pacing around her and starting back to the room. She followed her and saw that her daughter needed help. Faithfully now, Elaine reports each spell to the mother. The cat who was thrown out and abandoned, faithfully watches over her friend. Throw away cat.

My sister says that cats and dogs are angels sent here to help us to get through our lives. Are you throwing away an angel?

CUTEST PUPPY

Imagine this: you are the cutest puppy ever, and you live with your nine-month old mother and your ten five-week old siblings. Your half-grown mother was not spayed so the family could see the *miracle of birth*. You've started eating on your own and your owners are anxious to get rid of you because of the work you cause and the smell. You need to spend the next three weeks learning to be a dog, learning acceptable behaviours from your mother, but instead you are given to the first person who wants you - a young boy, no questions asked.

He takes you home, promises to look after you himself and your appealing cuddliness wins over the entire family. They keep you and you grow at an amazing rate. Somehow, you manage to house train yourself, but your need for exercise and stimulation leads you to chew in frustration, leaving the family almost barefoot. Because the boy has returned to his computer obsession and everyone is *too busy*, you have not been taught manners and do whatever you please. You get no exercise! You become an annoyance and so Dad ties you outside. You are confused, frightened and alone.

Someone comes to the door and you jump on them. Finally! Company! Then Dad moves you to the back of the yard, away from the house so you can't jump on visitors. You are devastated since you have been ousted from your pack. You begin to bark for your family, your pack. The next morning, someone walks down to your doghouse to give you water and food. Your chain has already spilled your previous water bowl, and you run through that muddy spot to greet your visitor. Like a good, submissive youngster, you try to lick his face, placing muddy footprints on his work clothes. He swears, shoves you away, drops your food and water and leaves. You bark in despair.

You're already much bigger than your mother and have a very loud voice. The next day, because of neighbours complaining, they put you in the car and drive you away from home. Excitement makes you pant and pace in the car. You drool, to the annoyance of your owners. They take you to a building filled with barking dogs.

You immediately sense desperation within the building. You jump on everyone you meet, looking for comfort and reassurance. You are the ninth large dog surrendered this week. You hear words like "behaviour problems" and "euthanasia", and "severe overcrowding." You hope that means some nice person will take you for a run in the fields until you are gloriously exhausted, and show you some affection.

Would your mother's owner now like to witness *the miracle of death*?

'TWAS THE NIGHT BEFORE CHRISTMAS

by Gertrude DunRoamin'

'Twas the night before Christmas and in the Vet Clinic basement
Sat twenty-two kitties - none with a placement.
"It's not that we're cold or lacking in care
It's just that it's Christmas and we're still all there!
Our coats, they're all soft, and look at that shine,
In hopes that a new friend soon would be mine!

We all dream of children, all snug in their beds
And visions of joining them dance in our heads"
While Frank walked past Basil with a hiss and a slap
We kittens all curled up - might as well take a nap

Then, in the upstairs there arose such a clatter
We all ran to the door to see what was the matter

The door slightly opened, Tic's through in a flash,
And running for Reception, when stopped by a crash!
The moon brightly shone through the room's only window
And gave a view of the vet, on her back, moaning "Oh!"
And then, close behind her stepping lively and quick
Well, just for a moment, I thought *'It's St Nick!'*

But it was her sister, who's so good to us.
"Get back in the basement, you cause such a fuss!
Now China, now Richard, now Ferris and Tac,
Now Snickers and Parker and Rogue - all get back!"
They were dressed all in parkas with boots on their feet
And they'd both made the trip to give us all a treat

Their faces were flushed, their eyes - they were blinking
I got the impression they might have been drinking!
They hugged me up close, made remarks 'bout my belly
And then filled our food bowls with treats - wet and smelly
They both looked so happy, so festive and merry
They cared not a whit that their clothes were all hairy

Then they spoke not a word as they both went to work
And cleaned out our litter boxes, then turned with a jerk
And tapping her finger on the side of my nose
And giving a nod, up the staircase they rose

Until Each One Has a Home

They'd patted our heads and hugged us all close
And reminded us all, what everyone here knows

'Cause we heard them exclaim as they each drove away
"We'll find you all homes - maybe just not today!"

BENTON REGINALD SEYMOUR BLACK

You should meet my newest favourite dog, Benny. Actually, we've named him Benton Reginald Seymour Black. And he is - black, I mean, with just a small white spot on his chest and on his toes. We're on a nickname basis now though, having spent a whole week together. He's big and black and soft (verging on flabby). His legs are heavily feathered and matted, and he smells a lot worse than my other canine residents (well, except maybe for Miles, but he rolled in skunk droppings and that's a whole other story). Despite his size and friendly nature, he's still frightened of new things, especially if he's not sure what I want or what I'm going to do with him.

He's slightly jumpier if approached from his blind side. Did I mention that one eye is small and shrivelled and occasionally seems to shine blue in a certain light? I think that is due to an injury that he's had from puppyhood. The other eye is a deep brown and shines too, but with intelligence, love and trust. The disparity in his eyes gives his craggy head a certain "Columbo-esque" expression. He rubs his face against my jeans as if I were his own private towel, and strangely, I feel somehow flattered and validated that this unsocialized, one-eyed, flabby, matted and smelly dog sticks closely by my side, wagging his tail for me, trusting me.

I am proud that we are friends after such a short acquaintance. He is frightened of many things, but now trusts me enough to take my word that he is safe. I have yet to convince him to chase a ball, but we did have a short game with a stick the other day. We've gone on a few walks, too, and he's prancing delightedly along with the other dogs, even leaving my side for short periods to investigate interesting smells.

He needs work, but it's mostly cosmetic and hormonal (he's not neutered yet). His life to date has been limited and sequestered, but he's risen to the challenge and has learned to relax in the rapidly-changing environment here and is getting used to *going to town*. He still has a few major hurdles to overcome - not the least of which includes another bath (maybe two), a neuter and a toenail trim, but I'm confident that we can see him through that without having to treat any post traumatic stress disorders as a result.

I think he'll clean up nicely, and his great personality will shine through more and more. Once he's acclimatized to a busy lifestyle and undergone his surgery (we'll deal with the eye, too, if necessary), I think he'll be ready for that special home - one with room to play, lots of activity, safe areas to explore and a permanent owner who deserves and respects the goodness in this dog. Meanwhile, he has me.

My brother, John, once told me about reading that when Europeans first came to America and asked the native people what kind of dog they had (meaning what breed), the answer most often given was "He's a *good* dog!"

That's Benton. He's a **good** dog!!

UNWANTED PETS

The other weekend we were on call for emergencies. I had just seen a tiny, emaciated kitten rescued from the brutal death suffered by his littermates. He was safe now, and as I tried to block the graphic mental image of the deaths of his siblings, I supplied contact numbers and information for reporting such behaviour to authorities.

Along with the usual client emergencies, DunRoamin' was kept busy with cases. Next, a stray cat, a beautiful young calico hit by a car was transported to the clinic, but was DOA. Shortly thereafter, a couple called regarding a dog who was lying on their lawn, would not get up, move or accept food or water. They suspected he had been hit by a car and had called everyone they knew to obtain help for him. They transported him to us and a glance told us that he was very old. We treated him and several days later, learned that he had been forcibly evicted from his home after a brutal beating for unwelcomed behaviour and was not allowed back. Gradually, over the next few days he seemed less and less painful and is now in foster care.

Then, we were called regarding a stray cat who, over the past week, was unable to eat. He was brought to the clinic. The odour of putrification and infection preceded him as he was carried inside. Severe infection and tissue damage was evident on one side of his mouth, bare bone jutting upward from his fractured jaw. As we attempted to clean the mess and assess the amount of damage, a metal object fell from his mouth, clanging onto our table. To our horror, a twenty-two bullet lay there - present in his mouth for a week!

Then, a beautiful young orange and white cat was brought in by a lady who had witnessed a blue Ford Tempo strike the cat and drive on. We named him Rhoan. Emergency treatment stabilized him, but could not prevent or repair the paralysis of his hind limbs from severe damage to his spinal cord. We had no option but euthanasia.

A phone call came next, from a lady who had found a kitten, all four legs tied together with twine, lying in a ditch with some garbage. The kitten seemed stable and alert, and she promised to seek medical examination for her new pet in the morning. She thanked us profusely for our advice and set out in search of the proper food for her little friend.

Finally, we had a call about a cat whose behaviour was preventing people from entering and leaving their house - she was in estrus (heat) and was pacing and yowling. Although DunRoamin' is not a shelter, they insisted on dropping this annoyance at the clinic (or else they would have her shot)

- a lovely young, unspayed silver tabby, healthy, not in need of medical care, easily managed if the compassion was there. They had the "You take it - it's your job!!" mentality.

> Unwanted kittens - killed with unbelievable cruelty.
> Unwanted cat - killed on the road.
> Unwanted dog - thrown into the street.
> Unwanted cat - shot in the face.
> Unwanted kitten - bound and thrown out with the garbage.
> Unwanted cat - no chance of care.

Overpopulation. Pets reproducing. Not enough homes. Unwanted pets. Suffering. What is the answer? The answer is to spay and neuter and to take responsibility for and care for your pets and the innocent, struggling lives out there. We need your help in finding ways to help these little guys and in preventing overpopulation. I'm asking you to be aware that we are not the only beings living here on this earth. I'm asking you to remember that ours are not the only lives with value. I'm begging you to remember that other species feel pain and cold and hunger and fear, just as you do. And I'm pleading with you to prove yourself a compassionate, caring person by helping the weaker and less fortunate, regardless of species, as we now approach the cold winter months. Please help prevent these cruelties. Please help the needy, and, as always, please spay and neuter.

"THEY'RE OKAY NOW!"

People often ask, "How do you stand it? The starving, abused, neglected and injured stray animals that you see, day after day?" That's a good question. It can be a very emotional time for all involved with DunRoamin' animals.

I am often incensed by the horrible circumstances that an innocent stray pet has had to endure. We all know that friendly, cuddly cats don't leave their warm homes in the dead of winter and walk to remote areas to establish new lives. How they get there is an obscene practice of some humans, a quick way to rid themselves of the results of their own failure to spay and neuter! They are thrown there, like trash, by people who should never have had animals in the first place.

Those cruel people should see the suffering that they have caused these poor innocent animals. They should be forced to look into the eyes of the lucky ones who get rescued by caring people who accidentally come across them and go out of their way to help. They should be forced to watch the shivering, desperate animal, weak from starvation. They should be forced to touch the body which is simply, now, fur over bones. They should see the gratitude in those innocent eyes, the relief at being warm, fed and safe. They should recognize the appalling cruelty of what they have done.

A friend has helped me to cope with my anger. As I would rant, "When I think of how that little thing lay there in pain for days . . . " he would interrupt with "But he's okay now! You have him, and you're looking after him. The past is past. He's safe with you and he's okay now."

That helps. I try not to think about their struggles with pain, trauma, cold and starvation prior to arriving at DunRoamin'. I know that now, my staff and volunteers will care for, love and pamper each one. They'll get heated food, hand fed if necessary, heated beds, cuddles, kisses and apologies for the damage the world has done to them. They'll get veterinary care and extra tender, loving care until "They're okay now!"

I think I'll make that our motto, "THEY'RE OKAY NOW!!" and emblazon it on a huge banner. They're safe, they're warm, they're fed, they're loved - smothered, almost - with love by our great staff and volunteers, trying to make up for their previous suffering and pain. And the new owners pledging to provide a warm, safe loving home forever. Even those whose lives we can't save with our medical abilities, the ones too sick, or too badly traumatized, they too, I believe, are in a safe, warm, loving home. They, too, are okay now.

ROGUE

I wish you all had had a chance to meet Rogue. He's the big grey and white tomcat, accidentally hit by a car at Tim Horton's in Florenceville a while ago. The horrified driver scooped him up immediately and brought him in for treatment. He had taken quite a wallop, with head injuries, a broken jaw, and severe trauma to one eye (we weren't sure it could be saved!)

We weren't sure, at first, if he was tame, but he submitted to our attentions as we cleaned his wounds and administered injections and eye ointments. His behaviour was exemplary. After a few days it became apparent that he was healing, and it seemed that he would be okay, provided DunRoamin' could afford to feed him! He dived into five cans of smelly wet food daily, and soon required a supplementary bowl of dry food on the side! After a couple of weeks we pronounced the eye healed and performed a quick neuter surgery.

Rogue was ready for adoption and was released into the basement with the other rescued cats. Although his face and ears bore the scars of some previous brawling, he politely moved in and began making friends. He was particularly good with the kittens, kindly sharing his canned food with them.

As his health improved, he began to play. We are used to the smooth, sleek, elegant cats inhabiting the basement, so the sight of this short-legged, rugged, strapping tom with seven toes on each giant foot playing with kittens never failed to make us smile.

At one point, it struck me that he walks like a cowboy, with calm, confident, measured steps and that insolent swagger of an arrogant gunslinger. I thought, *"He's the Clint Eastwood of the clinic basement, the Hoss Cartwright of the bonanza that is DunRoamin'!"* He has that barely controlled, serious appearance, that amazing strength and tenacious gaze of someone who fears nothing and no one, who takes what he wants when he wants it. And yet, all he wants is to be hugged and petted, to knead his huge front feet in response to a head and shoulder massage. That makes his day. He launches mock attacks at the tails of unsuspecting kittens and plays with their toys as if he was one of them.

He's a lover, not a fighter, and he loves not only all the clinic staff and all the kittens, but also all the soft cat food he's ever tried. It's not that he still requires supplemental soft food, he just loves it. He's served one can daily, and he still gets excited! In exact opposition to his appearance, he happily and quietly shares his windfall with the kittens. He's a big, swaggering, dangerous-looking pussycat who has stolen the hearts of all of his caregivers and all of the other cats as well.

Despite his rugged, tough, craggy, battle-scarred appearance, Rogue is not a cowboy, nor is he a rogue. Rough on the outside, he's soft and smooth on the inside. He's a real deep-down good cat. Remember the gunslinger movie "The Good, The Bad And The Ugly"? Well, our Rogue, he's the Good, not the Bad, and ... the Snuggly.

ABANDONED KITTENS
- DON'T LITTER

Well, it's happened once again. Kittens dropped off at a local shelter - ten of them, from what appear to be at least two litters. Faces covered with green secretions, eyes gummed shut, too young to be away from their mothers, covered with fleas, ears filled with earmite debris. On the up side, these kittens were left on the doorstep of a shelter. This sure beats throwing them in the woods or in the ditch, and we gratefully acknowledge that. We wonder where the mothers are - and we hope they are alright.

What you probably don't realize is that without the mothers, these kittens have little chance of survival even at the shelter, since there are not enough hands to meet their needs. These precious three- and four-week old kittens require feeding every few hours, as well as having their faces and eyes washed frequently to remove secretions. They need antibiotics and eye ointments. They suffer from viral illness which occurs in many unvaccinated cats, passed on to their offspring. They are weakened by their parasites

As the shelter staff was unable to manage so many needy little guys on top of their huge commitment to their other animals, DunRoamin' Stray and Rescue and Florenceville Veterinary Clinic staff and volunteers have taken them on. Hopefully all will survive. Again, I thank the person who dropped those little guys - now named Riggs, Wilson, Murdoch, Farrah, Caprice, Lionel, Calista, Evelyn, Leroy and Burbank - at the shelter. The staff called for help right away and we were able to prevent dehydration and protect them from illnesses that they might pick up at the shelter. They "cleaned up pretty good," and now after 10 days of treatment and support they are playing and starting to purr. Dunroamin' is elated!

Some may be thinking "What's the big deal? Just get rid of them! They are a dime a dozen!" But – think about this. When you stand up in church and sing "He sees the little sparrow fall", do you think He doesn't see what happens to these animals? Do you think He doesn't care?

Now, we just have to raise funds to vaccinate, deworm and spay and neuter all these little guys before they can find homes *-if* they can find homes, since cats are not in short supply. DunRoamin' alone has over one hundred in our care.

Consider the advantages of spaying your cats - stop kitten suffering and stop proliferation of unwanted cats and kittens.

HOW MANY BLOWS IS "UNDUE"?

Having read some of the rhetoric surrounding the brutal bludgeoning deaths of the tiny dogs in Minto, NB, I can't help but notice the political response to the concerns of the public. It seems to centre around dangerous dog legislation, leash laws, dog taxes and kennel licencing. The only response that bears even a little merit in the above context is the marked increase in licencing for dogs that are not spayed or neutered. Assuming that licences are obtained, they would be much more expensive for unaltered dogs, potentially giving some incentive for spaying and neutering. It does not, however, address the cat overpopulation issues.

It also does not get to the crux of public concerns. We need laws to protect animals from **us**. Do we consider our lives more worthy, our pain more severe, our suffering more valid than the innocent products of our failure to manage our pets' reproduction? Do we condone bludgeoning, starvation, abandonment, drowning or shooting our pets as a means of disposing of them without "undue pain?" (What is "undue pain"? One hammer blow? Two? Bleeding to death from multiple misplaced bullets? I have four dogs with bullets still embedded in their bodies, rescued from puddles of blood in ditches.)

Are we not yet a civilized society? Do we still deem these sentient animals as property to be disposed of at the owner's whim and method of choice? Where is the compassion, the empathy, the righteousness of this attitude?

And where are our law-makers that they have left us so ineffective and helpless that we cannot even seek justice for five innocent beings, bludgeoned to death in front of the very officials whose job it is to protect them? And a five hundred dollar fine? On the market, each little dog would have sold for at least that so it will be easy to recoup that money with the sale of his next litter! And our Baptist minister, who brutally killed these little dogs - has he heard that "He sees the little sparrow fall"? He may plan to go to heaven, but me? If that's where he goes, I want to go where the dogs are!

BONES

A while ago we received a very painful reminder of the reason DunRoamin' exists. A distressed young woman burst into the clinic carrying a box containing a blanket-wrapped object.

"We found him by the road," she said. "He's so cold and has a big cut on his neck, and he's so thin!" She had had previous dealings with DunRoamin' and was aware of our mandate to help unowned, seriously ill strays. Still, she tried her best to take some responsibility for his care. "We don't have any money," she confessed, "but we do have this stack of Co-Op cash and Canadian Tire money. Maybe you can use that for food and stuff?"

Under the blanket lay a very sick, extremely emaciated young cat, unable to stand, ears, legs, tail and feet severely frost-bitten, body temperature thirty four degrees Celsius. Anything less than thirty five degrees Celsius will not sustain life. He also had a five centimetre laceration on his neck exposing his jugular vein and windpipe.

"He's just bones!" his vet whispered. His coat was rough and unkempt. Pus had caked under his chin and around his neck and chest - drainage from his terrible wound. He was skin over bones. He also felt gritty to the touch because of all of the fleas crawling on his little body.

Clinic staff (who are also all DunRoamin' volunteers) immediately abandoned their lunches and disappeared in different directions. One staff member placed him on heating pads. Another started an IV to infuse warm fluids. One gave him emergency drugs, someone removed the debris from his nostrils to allow easier air flow, and someone gave pain medication for his painful frostbite. Someone gave him a pill which immediately kills fleas, he was crawling with them. Someone started antibiotics, and someone hovered over him, gently petting his head, telling him how everything would be "okay now."

Much later in the day, he had improved enough to dive, nose first, into warm food. With continued treatment and careful monitoring, he was able to sit up by day's end, also devouring multiple and frequent small meals. And today? Well, today, he purred! He's able to stand now, and eats everything in sight. And he's had a bath (the water ran red from the flea debris). He smells much better now, too.

Today, we all feel better. Today we think "Bones" will make it, although he will need several weeks of convalescence.

Yesterday and today, DunRoamin' did what DunRoamin' is meant to do. DunRoamin' cared for an injured cat who had no other options, who required intensive veterinary care, who overcame the odds and who thanked us in a purrfectly delightful way.

This was a real DunRoamin' case - an innocent young cat, struggling desperately to survive cold, starvation and injury, outdoors and alone, found by caring people just in time to save his life.

He's all done roamin' now.

DO YOU KNOW WHERE YOUR PET IS?

It's a cold night! Do you know where your dog or cat is?

Is he safely ensconced in your warm house, as he should be? Or is he outside, shivering, curled into a tight ball trying to preserve his body heat? Is he alone in the cold, trying to keep warm, while you bask in the warmth of your house and its fireplace? Does he fight winter alone? If he must be outside (I can't think of any really good reason), is he in a well-insulated, proper-sized dog house that will preserve his body heat and prevent drafts? Does your dog live through the winter as your companion or does he merely survive the winter, lonely and cold at the far corner of your lot?

If you check with any animal welfare organization - from the NBSPCA right on up to the American SPCA, PETA, Dumb Friends League, Best Friends Shelter, and Dogs Deserve Better, you will find total agreement. In this day and age, given the advancement society has made over the years in understanding animals and the acceptance of pets as family members who feel the same discomforts that we do, dogs and cats should be housed indoors, especially during the winter months. No longer is it considered acceptable (in fact, it is considered cruelty) to chain your dog to a flimsy doghouse at the far corner of your lot and feed him once daily. Nor is it acceptable to allow him to run at large. You, who adopted this amazing, sentient, intriguing and loving species (dog or cat), owe that creature certain things. They include:

1. the right to live a life, free of pain, hunger, cold, fear and boredom;

2. the right to exercise to allow them to experience some semblance of the roles that they were developed (by man) to fulfill;

3. the right to be part of a family or pack (as nature intended) and to be spared the pain of intense loneliness;

4. the right to be valued for their uniqueness, their beauty, their perfectness. (Look closely at the next cat you see - notice how perfectly it is formed, how amazing its colours are, how perfect its face. Respect its place here on earth. We all have the same maker;) and finally

5. the right not to be born until they can be assured of a home and family to protect them, and the right to live as long as they are physically able to enjoy life— Not to be born until their bodies are precious and men have ceased to exploit them because they are cheap and plentiful!

George Bernard Shaw wrote: *"The worst sin toward our fellow creatures is not to hate them, but to be indifferent to them. That is the essence of inhumanity."*

Please make sure your pet has adequate shelter, food, and water that can't freeze if he's outside for any amount of time at all. It is only proper.

LITTLE JOE HENRI

Hi there! My name must be Little Joe Henri now. At least they call me Henri here. I was living on the street of Arthurette before. People said I was something called "abandoned." What does "abandoned" mean? I know that suddenly I had no home, the people I lived with and loved were gone, and there was nothing to eat and nowhere to sleep. I know I was very hungry, and huddled, shivering, under trees and in ditches for a long time, and it was so dark and cold at night! I was terrified, and did not know what to do. Some people started chasing me, and I didn't know them and I was frightened. Would they hurt me? I was very hungry. Then a man started leaving food out for me. It was so *good*!! After a long time, I got trapped in his garage and some women put me in a car and took me to something called "DunRoamin." What's a "DunRoamin'?"

Then something called a veterinarian put me on a table, put water and stuff in my ears (they were so itchy and smelly) and cleaned them. Then it put stuff in my ears to make them feel better. It also did something called vaccinating and deworming before it put me in its car and drove me to another house. It was the strangest place I've ever seen and it smelled like a dozen dogs lived there. Then the veterinarian became a person. She fed me, introduced me to all the other dogs, and gave me a warm soft bed to lie on. It felt so nice to feel safe and warm after sleeping in the ditches. She said that I looked like a small Shar pei with a wispy Cocker Spaniel's head (whatever they are). Then she laughed and said that must make me a Shocker Pei-niel. Her friend said that whatever I was, I was small and ugly - so ugly that I was cute! She said I was a good dog.

I must confess to being quite smitten by this veterinarian thing. I was scared and cold and wary of the other dogs at first. She held me in her arms until I stopped shaking, then she set me on the floor and said "You're a dog!" I guess I must be. I look more like them than I do people, although some people have a lot of wrinkles on their heads and necks like I do.

A few days later I went to work with her. She said I was going to be "tutored" and I would be so smart. I felt funny when I came home with her again, like I'd slept the whole time I was at her work. It also felt funny when I walked, but it didn't hurt or anything. They wouldn't let me run and play with Nigel (another fellow here) for a few days, and talked about something called an "incision."

I'm allowed to play now, and I love Nige, even if he is five times my size. He said he came here because he had a broken leg and his family couldn't help him. He likes it here, and his leg is all better now. I'm glad, 'cause I've been biting all his legs and I wouldn't like to bite a broken one. Nige said he slept all day one time at work too, and he felt funny walking for awhile, too. He thought it was just his cast.

I heard them say I was a "Foster" dog. I thought I was a "Henri" dog. They keep changing my name. Whatever!

I like it here. I'm safe and warm and they hug and pet me a lot. I feel safe, so I'm not going to worry. Guess I'll go play with Nigel - I really like Nige.

Love,

Foster or Henri or Whatever

DUNBREEDIN'

You know, I've been thinking. Now that DunRoamin' has garnered more interest and community support, it may be time for me to start another organization. This one would be a grass roots, fundamentalist, card-carrying extremist group whose mandate would be to change public perception and acceptance of the indiscriminate and unnecessary breeding of pets. I'd call the off-shoot group "DunBreedin'," and its goal would be to decrease animal suffering and homelessness, but by attacking a different aspect of the problem from that of DunRoamin'. Our cards would read "***DunBreedin' - until every pet has a good home.***"

DunBreedin' would be lead by an enigmatic, charismatic, opinionated, sincere, slightly off-beat but essentially altruistic person. I will study the techniques of indoctrination and use cult methods to influence my followers to embrace and preach our beliefs: "Spaying and neutering pets decreases suffering."

The followers will travel from house to house expounding at great length on the injustices perpetrated on the innocent and offering advice on prevention of suffering and respect for life.

DunBreedin' would strike pre-emptively at the breeding of pet animals. DunBreedin' would advocate for spays and neuters of all pet animals by six months of age. This would stop the abandonment, the abuse, the starvation and the suffering of the hapless, unwanted progeny of people's pet cats and dogs. This would also relieve the animal shelters of the horrific chore of euthanizing (i.e. killing) homeless, unwanted, healthy, loving, beautiful animals. Do you think that doesn't happen here in rural NB? Think again! Ask the local shelter workers and veterinarians who are forced to be involved in that obscenity. Ask them if it affects their sleep.

But DunBreedin'! If that could just change people's mind set, stop them from breeding unwanted animals, from producing more pets than there are available homes - think of the suffering that would be prevented (pets, vets and shelter workers)!

It is the obvious solution. Following the laws of supply and demand - obviously, right now supply is overwhelming demand, leaving pet offspring with little value to consumers. Reverse it! Decrease the supply, and the value (and therefore level of care) goes up, suffering goes down. It's that simple!

Yes, that's the solution. "Don't breed your animals until every pet has a good home!" That's DunBreedin'!

And I'm DunWritin'.

STRAY THOUGHTS

You would think at my age, that I'd have a lot more answers than questions, wouldn't you? You'd think that I would grow wiser with each passing year. I'm sure that happens with some people, but, unfortunately, not with me. I'm one of those people who are struck with the "The more you know, the more you know you don't know" syndrome. Or, perhaps, said more succinctly, "Ignorance is bliss."

Some questions that keep me awake at night are innocuous, some very profound. One such question is: Will a cat rat you out, or just pussyfoot around the situation? Another is: What does an animal think when asked to pause for a moment? And if kittens are thrown in a ditch, do we call that kitty litter?

Other questions plague me - and if I'm plagued by questions, should I feel sick about it? Seriously though, if a dog barks his head off while you are gone, how does he get it seamlessly back in place by the time you arrive home?

How can you have one Siamese cat? (And, if they were separated as babies, are they still Siamese?)

If you have a "dog day afternoon" does it become a "three dog night?" Just asking! Do middle-aged female cats go through "meownopaws?" And is that why they are so grouchy? Probably. Why do we say "The cat's out of the bag?" If the cat's out of the bag at my office, it's being pursued through the clinic, and at least one person is bleeding!

Am I doggedly looking for answers, or just being catty? I don't know. Maybe I've just been working too hard. The one thing I know from writing this is that I'm not getting any wiser.,

And, one more thing. When you have stray thoughts, are they always about animals? Mine are.

NOT A TIME TO KILL

(An Open Letter To The Owners Of the Grey & White Kitten)

Imagine a small cat, a mere kitten, sitting in the yard at the home where he was born, near Glassville, NB. His mother is close by, interacting with the people who live there, who brought the mother home as a kitten. He is the last of her third litter in the two years of her life. She's never seen a vet. The kitten doesn't approach the people. He's not exactly afraid of them. He knows they occasionally bring food, but he's never been handled, and he's never played with them.

Further, imagine that one of the people suddenly grabs the kitten and stuffs him into a box, swiftly closing the cover and throwing this box into a car.

The car motor starts, further scaring the little guy, and he feels the strange movement of the vehicle. He hunkers into the darkness of the box, hoping that the very darkness hides him from the roaring monster. After a time, he sees light as the box opens and a huge smelly hand grabs his squirming little body and pulls him from his hiding place into the full light. He sees a blur outside the windows – he's never experienced this movement before, or the rough handling by the person. He tries to hold on with all his claws, but the person curses and holds him dangling by the scruff of his neck. He is so helpless and terrified. The window opens and he feels the draft and the roar of the wind on his face. What's going on?

The car slows, and from the corner of his eye he sees what looks like a mud puddle – only much bigger. Suddenly, with a sharp pain in his back, he feels himself airborne, high above the tall roadside grasses. Then, with an agonizing thud, he lands on his face on the hard, rocky roadside. He hears a "snap" and knows that his jaw is broken, feels the skin tear away from his lower jaw and rip away from the side of his nose and upper lip.

He is stunned by the pain, paralyzed with fear. His head aches profoundly, and his face and jaw are on fire with pain. He has never been so frightened. He sits where he lands, dizzy, panting and nauseated, fighting for composure. Blood streams from his nose and mouth as he struggles to breathe. He knows many of his front teeth are gone, smashed from their deep sockets. He sits. He can't move.

Then he hears a soft voice. "Oh, my gosh! It's okay, little guy. I'll help you." Gentle hands lift him into another car. A soft voice talks continuously, gentle hands cradle him as he feels the car move forward. The trembling hands comfort him. "I'll get help for you," the soft voice promises. "It will be okay."

He is driven to a veterinarian who struggles to see past the horror of what has been done to him, and prepares a treatment plan to help him. Analgesics take away the pain, and he gratefully relaxes. Surgical repair re-aligns his upper and lower jaws and cosmetic surgery repairs his torn face. He is medicated, fed, comforted, fussed over, and in two days begins to eat a liquid diet on his own. Caregivers smile proudly. The swelling over his eyes subsides, finally allowing him to see again.

Visitors come and go, exclaiming over the atrocity that has been perpetrated against him. Are some of them crying? He hears his caregivers gratefully thank a lady who makes a large donation to help pay for his care. He thinks that maybe most people are good, that his people are not the norm. As he learns to enjoy a cuddle, he hears people mention Wednesday Addams and gleans from conversations that a similar vicious occurrence badly damaged her face last year. People begin to call him Pugsley – after Wednesday's brother in the Addams Family TV show. He identifies anger and despair in the voices of his caregivers, and he understands now, that what happened to him was bad. Cruel. Hateful. Inhumane.

Now – imagine that you are that kitten!

HOGAN

I must tell you about Hogan. He's a DunRoamin' dog, a nine-month-old Border Collie pup. He was acquired from very substandard conditions by a family who surrendered him to DunRoamin' after twenty-four hours. He had spent every waking moment herding their toddlers. Still, there was no way they would consider returning him to the conditions from which he had come. I'm fostering Hogan.

He's beautiful - tall and lean, tri-coloured with a mostly white face, right eye covered by a black patch and brown trim. I was immediately drawn to him (well, he is a dog!) and was impressed by his intelligence and willingness to please. I love the sheer goodness of that pup and his complete willingness to co-exist with the other dogs and the clinic cats. He's a natural at cuddling. He has energy to burn, though, and although he's been here a month, I still marvel at his energy level (typical for a Border Collie).

Let me describe his average day.

Hogan is up at the crack of dawn and needs breakfast. We feed him and the eight others. I stay near Hogan, as he forgets to eat if something attracts his attention. I constantly remind him to eat before someone else eats his food. He then goes out into the large fenced-in field and plays with his best friend, Nigel. He herds Nige, nipping at his heels for as long as Nigel tolerates it. An hour or so later, I bring Nigel in for a rest and put Seven, the Siberian Husky, out to play. Later, I replace Seven with Miles, the Border Collie mix, and then replace him with Easy, the Pitt mix. Having had a great romp, the others nap. Hogan digs a few more holes in the already mutilated lawn, chews on a bone, then amuses himself (and me) by dropping a ball over the side of the deck, then racing around to the stairs, off the deck and down the hill, catching the ball before it stops rolling. He does this repeatedly, pausing occasionally to throw the ball in the air, pounce on it and continue his game. I think, "What a love of life!" as I fill in today's gaping holes and smooth the soil. Hogan paces nearby, trying to figure out what he can do to help.

I call him inside, thinking we'll start obedience training. One half hour later, I say, "Sit." His bum is on the floor before the T resonates. I try a recall – "Hogan, Come!" My hair lifts from my face and neck with the speed of his arrival, his eyes expectantly holding mine, expression saying, "Anything else?" I wonder if I can teach him to vacuum up dog hair?

It's evening, getting dark, and Hogan is playing in the living room with Nigel. We actively discourage this, since we now have few decorative touches remaining in the room. Hogan rests his head on my friend's knee. He says, "Go ask your foster-mudder!" Hogan puts his head on my knee, looking me in the eye, expression hopeful. I open my arms. "Okay, Hogan." He leaps onto my lap, wiggles onto his back, head on my shoulder, and completely relaxes, legs splayed, abdomen exposed, eyes closed, almost instantly asleep. We are so close. I smile slightly as I wonder if I am one of Hogan's heroes.

I support him until my arm aches, marveling at his complete trust and innocence and his deep untroubled sleep. I gaze inwardly and wonder, *"How will I sleep tonight?"*

TATER TOTS

Dumped in an abandoned potato house, they were immediately dubbed the "Tater Tots" - four little kittens, bruised, dry, scabby, sides hollow, parasitized, cold, eyes obscured by secretions, afflicted with disease. The Clinic looked like a MASH unit, with staff clumped around each small fry, attending to their medical needs. Staff was boiling and the sheer brutality of the situation grated on the nerves of the animal lovers.

Whoever left those little guys there should be skinned. They had dropped those kittens like hot potatoes. I doubt that they will sprout wings anytime soon. I, personally, have wished a blight upon their heads, and that they be infested with aphids. (We know that you harvest what you sow.)

The four little sweet potatoes, Spud and Yukon Gold (the boys) and Shepody and Tater (the girls) have now become warmed-up couch potatoes, and we've whipped up nourishing meals for them. They are growing like bad weeds and would love to be stored in loving homes before they're too old to cut the mustard anymore. They're not superfries, they're just homefries!

Some people might consider it a strange notion, but I think that when we meet the International Harvester, He will separate the seed from the rotten ones. Some will go up the big conveyor belt, some will be culls.

ALL DOGS GO TO HEAVEN

While Christmas shopping the other day, a DVD caught my eye (it had dogs on it) entitled "All Dogs Go To Heaven."

"Yes," I thought. *"Of course they do, and most cats too!"* (Although I have noted some questionable cat behaviour in my work place - painful cat behaviour!) Who is worthier of a heaven than dogs - with their complete and total love, their goodness, their non-judgmental loyalty, their ability to forgive, their work and their companionship. As my mind continued its wandering in this vein, I eventually concluded that all dogs *do not* go to Heaven, at least not here on earth. Some go in a very different direction. Some go to uncaring and neglectful homes and suffer endlessly. Some live cold, lonely, restricted, hungry, thirsty and boring lives on the end of chains, severely lacking in the basic necessities of life. Others are abused and neglected from puppyhood - often under the very noses of unobservant neighbours.

Take Sophia, for instance. This little waif was found in a ditch, so badly matted that she could not walk, one leg bent at an abnormal and painful angle and held there by her mats, the trapped leg raw with devitalized flesh allowing bone to be visible. The smell! Infected leg, infected ears, filth, matted coat, excreta caked in her coat. Terrified. Distrustful.

It was necessary to clip her entire body and then she underwent skin grafting and reconstructive surgery to cover the gaping wounds on her foreleg. What about her gaping psychic wounds?

And then, there's Brad, the Pitt mix puppy- abused, terrified of the touch of a human hand, one eye so painful and so badly injured that it had to be removed. Who abuses and injures ten-week-old puppies? Who makes them cringe and duck from a human hand? Who makes that tiny pup so terrified that he feels he must fight for his very life? At ten weeks old!

"He's okay now," as we say, and he's learning that hands mean treats and cuddles and pats and toys. That should have been the first thing he learned. To think that we are trying to rehabilitate a ten-week-old pup . . .

And Sophia - she's a sweetheart, and I'll bet that she thinks she's gone to Heaven already. She's definitely traded up - way up! She's been adopted by a wonderful person who is trying to make up for the suffering in her past. Sophia's more than "okay now." She's got it made!

And Brad? He's making more friends daily and starting to play like a puppy should. Sadly, he'll live his entire life with only one eye, but he'll be okay when he gets that great home he deserves.

It has been said that, properly trained, a man can be dog's best friend. I believe that, and would love to find a suitable training manual.

Robert Louis Stephenson said, *"You think dogs will not be in heaven? I tell you, they will be there long before any of us!"* I agree!

The DunRoamin' Vet's Christmas

"On the first day of Christmas, DunRoamin' sent to me - a tomcat that couldn't even pee!"

I'll skip the repetition and jump to the last verse now.

"On the 12th day of Christmas, DunRoamin' sent to me:

12 traffic traumas
11 frozen felines
10 hoarder's victims
9 ringwormed Ragdolls
8 Labs a-limping
7 cats a-bandoned
6 scuzzy kittens
5 Goldendoodles
4 squalling pups
3 cast-off collies

Mildred A. Drost DVM

2 beaten Boxers
and a tomcat who couldn't even pee!!!"

**Merry Christmas from the Friends
and Strays Of DunRoamin'!**

THANKS

As you all know, Border collies are the Einsteins of the dog world. For this reason (my amazing intellect) I, Hogan, have been selected to pen a heartfelt "Thank you" to our benefactors.

DunRoamin' strays and rescues owe a great debt of gratitude to the many, many people who have helped in our treatment, housing, care, and efforts to find us safe, warm homes. This includes, but is not limited to, those who go out of their way to get help for us, those who care for, cuddle, medicate, treat and clean up after us on a never-missed, often daily, basis, those who raise funds for treatments and food, those who foster us, those who use their own talents to comfort us, those who pray for us, and those who openly discourage, object to and publicize the less-than-humane treatment of us.

Those people are forming an animal-friendly community where more and more members are speaking out against neglect and abuse. There is less tolerance for the people who intentionally cause suffering. Life is easier for us.

From the bottom of our hearts, we, the rescued, thank:

> those who see hunger and thirst, and seek to alleviate it (not cause it or accept it);
>
> those who see fear and anxiety, and choose to calm it (rather than cause it or try to gain power from it);
>
> those who see suffering and try to find help for it (rather than ignore it or be the cause of it);
>
> those who see cold and try to provide much-needed warmth (rather than exclude living beings from desperately needed heat);
>
> those who recognize that suffering and despair are not only restricted to human animals (and try to help - human and animal alike); and
>
> those who see that a life is a life, and realize that that life deserves to be lived as well as possible (rather than exist, suffering, waiting for release).

Those are the ones who deserve the thanks, and whom we do thank.

As we often say amongst ourselves, as DunRoamin' animals: our lives have become purrrfectly comfortable and arf-fully, arf-fully wonderful with your kind help and care. We are having a ball in our new, safe homes. (Ball? Ball? Did someone say "BALL"? Where? WHERE? I mean...., ahem,

ahem. That wasn't me! Ahh, I digress!) We are enjoying our safe, secure, loving surroundings and remain eternally grateful for your timely interventions and support.

Respectfully submitted,

Hogan

Fight Terrierism

Dogs! Know this! We at the Clinic and at DunRoamin' do *not* negotiate with terriers. Not any factions! Not Yorkies, not Silkies, not Jack Russells, and *not* Pitts! Not Cairns, not even Bostons. None! We will not change our position! We will not negotiate!

Since the beginning of the tailban, we have been pressured to change. We will not! Our national association has taken a stand against tail docking as well as ear cropping. We will abide by their direction. You will need to resign yourselves to living with your God-given appearance. We will not do your cosmetic surgeries! You are cute enough as you are! You should not be primarily focused on appearance! You should be focused on being good dogs!

You must return our shoes, our socks, our gloves and other belongings. We will not pay ransom! Brad, the Pitt - I want my stethoscope back - also the stolen syringes and other office supplies. I don't want to know what you are doing with them— I just want them back!

There will be no more blitz attacks on our ankles! You will no longer chew holes in our clothes! You will *not* urinate in our homes. We will not tolerate it! In retaliation, we will feed you cheap dog food, remove all your Kong toys and balls, and no longer allow you to sleep on our furniture. We'll hold back on your bacon-flavoured treats and your chewies!

This is our position. We are immovable! You live in our world, abide by our laws!

FREE DOG

I've been noticing, lately, many ads on the classifieds, and on the net and Facebook, dealing with attempts to place pets. The most heartbreaking and anger provoking have been two ads that want to place older pets. One pictures a lovely dog lying on the floor with a child, and the ad states that the dog must go because "he runs and I hate that!"

Once I get my anger in check, I then start to wonder "Is the dog neutered? Have these brilliant people tried to teach him to stay home? Do they know anything about dog behaviour? Does the dog even have a reason to want to stay home?" (Doesn't sound like he's well-loved or even well-thought of.)

After nine years of living with someone, and loving them as only a dog can, this family wants to give him to a stranger because "He won't stay home!" How's that for commitment.

That dog could be taught to stay home or enticed to stay with his family if his hormones weren't drawing him out to find the girls. He would likely willingly stay home with people who have concern or respect for him and who teach him the things that he needs to know. Dogs don't come all trained and knowing everything that is required of them. They take work and commitment.

As my grandfather always said "In order to train a dog, you have to know more than the dog does!" That means that you may need help from an experienced trainer to find the right way to teach your dog the things that you want him to know. Think of it like this – do you know how to fly planes, train horses, teach school, or make pottery. Those are all things that need to be learned – as do proper methods of dog training. Get help - don't just give up and throw your family member to some stranger.

Learn to respect your dog for his goodness. Respect his life! He is not trash to be thrown away when you are finished with him. He is a unique, aware, knowing creature with thoughts, feelings and strong family ties. He is a pack creature and, for better or for worse, you are his pack. Think about what you are doing to him with your "Free dog" ads and think about what will happen to him as you hustle him out and into the care of a stranger – after nine years of loving your family.

I hope you know how to explain your actions to him – I don't!

THE DOG WHO CAME IN FROM THE COLD

This is an account of a dog who did not need much from DunRoamin'. He had his own friends. He is a young German Shepherd who was abandoned by his reputedly abusive owner. That dog lived for almost two years on his own, with no home.

Initially, he was glimpsed on the edge of a forested area near the town, and concerned residents began leaving food out for him. "Forest," as they called him (because he lived, well... in the forest) was too shy and nervous to allow anyone to touch him, but gradually began to recognize and show himself to his friends who appeared each day with his food. Still, he could not allow himself to be touched. Over time, Forest ventured closer to the town, until early in the winter he was seen near the school grounds while children were playing. Concerns were voiced about the children's safety.

Residents were divided. Some advocated a complete de-Forestation project, if you will, while his friends strongly believed in a sustainable Forest-protection approach.

The second group, joined by other like-minded individuals, rallied around their friend and committed to bringing Forest back in. They were already concerned about his ability to withstand the winter cold. One resident rented a live trap built for dogs; two others offered a home, if Forest was adoptable. The village itself offered to pay for Forest's training and rehabilitation.

As it turned out, Forest was live-trapped and allowed himself to be handled, fear evident, but no aggression. He was taken to DunRoamin' to be assessed for health and temperament. Within hours, Forest was relaxed and enjoying a good belly-rub and the first warmth and security in many, many months.

If there was a problem with Forest, it was that he didn't want to go *out!* He was quickly leash-trained, neutered, vaccinated and eagerly adopted by one of his long-time benefactors. His friend picked him up from the pet hospital in the truck that he always drove when he fed Forest - so that Forest would recognize him.

A relieved Forest, now renamed "Roamen," is now safely ensconced in his forever home with his delighted new family. Kudos to the town for their long-term caring and concern for this canine resident, and to his friends for their commitment to his wellbeing - again proving that De-Forestation is *not* an acceptable answer!

BORN TO LOSE

That's what will happen to many of the kittens born to pet cats this spring. They lose. Cats - loving, friendly, beautiful and intelligent cats are euthanized every day at shelters because there is nowhere for them to go. Those may be the luckier ones. With cat breeding season upon us - again, ardently, DunRoamin' asks cat owners to have their animals spayed and neutered. Please do not allow them to breed and bring more unwanted cats into an already overcrowded world. Most of those litters of kittens will lose.

They will lose their lives due to starvation, parasitism, cold, predators, disease and trauma. They will not find safe, secure homes. There are not enough homes out there to care for the cats now living, let alone those to be born this spring.

"How do we know?" you think. "I found homes for my last litter." But - were they good, safe, permanent homes? Or did they end up like the suffering cats DunRoamin' sees almost daily? Did they take homes other desperate cats need? Did they end up like our strays? Did they *become* our strays??

Did they end up losing their eyes due to injury or disease like Mosey, Cromwell, Drucilla, Bruce, Ashton and One-Eyed Jake?

Did they lose limbs like Maggie, Sweets and Bixby? Did they lose their breath, struggling painfully for every bit of oxygen they could pull into their infected, injured or collapsed lungs, like Cyrus, GC and Bones?

Did they lose their ears like Mercedes, Winslow and Bones?

Were their tails broken and lost due to lack of circulation and injury like Val, Bones, Jewel and Glen?

OR - did they simply lose their lives like Cyrus, Ruffles, Denzel, Burbank, Rhoan, Maple, Sweets and Makita - too badly damaged by a world in which pet owners have carelessly allowed an overpopulated species to breed uncontrolled?

Born to lose!

ROMEOW

Have you heard about this injured stray? Found at the side of the road, thin, travel-worn, injuries to all four legs, this battle-scarred warrior has been named "Romeow." Why, you might wonder? Well, think about it. Young intact male cat, cat breeding season, hormone-driven, looking for his Julie-cat - any Julie-cat. And based on the battle scars in various stages of healing - some fresh, some old, some chronic, some unable to heal - my guess is that Romeow has been running on hormones (and only hormones if his visible ribs and hip bones are any indication) for quite some time now.

Thankfully for him, despite his filthy appearance and the strong odour of infection, he was saved from the ditch, brought to the clinic and treated for his injuries, his malnutrition and his infections, then neutered, vaccinated and dewormed. After plastic surgery to cover one gaping leg wound, he'll be ready to settle down, we hope, with or without his Julie-cat.

Until Each One Has a Home

In thinking of his plight and his rescue, potential dialogues haunt me, thanks to Mrs. Carter, my high school English teacher. Such conversations as these plague my thoughts:

"Romeow, Romeow, wherefore art thou, Romeow?
"I'm in the ditch, I've hurt my leg!"

And as he is being transported for medical care: "But soft! What light through yonder window breaks?"
"'Tis the workplace of the local vet! She awaits within, so as to treat thine wounds."

And to the vet: "How severe dost thou assess my wounds?"
"You and I are past our dancing days, Romeow!"

"Wow, Romeow, you really smell rank!"
"A rose by any other name would smell as sweet!"

"Now, Romeow, thou must breathe the gases so that thou wilst not feel the thrust of the knife as I repair thy wounds and complete thy neuter."
"Goodnight, goodnight. Parting is such sweet sorrow."

"Vet, what hast thou done to me? Thou hast ruint my life! I thought you said 'tutor!!'
A plague on both your houses!"

"Romeow, thou must live here with the basement cats until thy body hast healed!"

"Romeow is finished! There is no end, no limit, measure bound, in that words death. No words can that woe sound. Never was seen so black a day as this!

O woeful day!"
"Oh, Romeow, it's just a neuter! It's
not like your life is over!"

Another tragedy of Shakespearian proportions - one that a quick neuter at five months of age would have easily averted.

DIXON

Not long ago, I said goodbye to my old friend, Dixon. It was hard - as it should be. I hadn't known him very long, but he was old, and we quicky became close friends. Apparently he'd been seen near the road in a town north of here, for a week. Someone finally called for assistance for him and he was brought to us by Animal Control since he was so emaciated and dehydrated that he couldn't stand!

I thought, "Why would he stay in one place until he was that badly off, and that dehydrated?" Emergency treatment and food improved his condition somewhat, but test results answered my nagging questions. He had stayed in that one area for a week because his heart condition was so bad he did not have the strength to leave, or to get water.

In medical terms, he had a pericardial effusion, likely due to a heart-base tumour. Effectively, his heart could not pump properly, leaving him very weak. Sadly, his condition could not be rectified. Even sadder, there was no owner, no family to attend to him. It didn't seem right that he would struggle alone for a week, struggle to respond to our treatments, and then be euthanized when his two days were up with Animal Control. Yes, his time was short! No, he couldn't exercise, but he could walk outside to do his business, and he did enjoy socializing with his avid admirers at the clinic. He worried, though, when he went outside, that he would not be allowed back in.

I heard myself say, "I'll take him home until he's ready to go. I'll make the time." And so I did. For ten days Dixon stayed with me, impressing me with his good manners, his acceptance of the other dogs, his good hygiene, and his wonderful personality. He showed me love, gratitude, friendship, humour, stoicism, gentleness and dignity. He showed me that he was a class act - a *good* dog.

I enjoyed my short time with Dixon, trying my best to be his family. We made pancakes with real maple syrup for him. He loved them! I cooked up some Kraft Dinner, and his friends at the clinic sent him mashed potatoes, gravy and chicken fingers from the Village Grill. He ate Timbits and Tim's biscuits and one of Gary's muffins from Magan Services. He had Milk Bones and rawhides and even half of my Oatmeal Crisp at breakfast. We hugged and petted him any time he wanted it, spent quality time with him, and when he was ready to go, we said goodbye, shortly after his favourite meal of pancakes and maple syrup.

As he prepared to leave, we repeated, over and over, a message sent from his friends at the clinic, a message in which we strongly believed: "Good boy, Dixon, good boy! You're a good boy, Dixon."

LOUP

Have I told you about my friend Loup (we pronounce it "Lou")? She came to us years ago, before DunRoamin' had a name. She'd been shot - twice in the chest and once near the nerve bundle that supplies her right front leg. She was thin, her foot pads were worn, she couldn't stand, and she had been recently nursing puppies, even though she did not appear to be more than a year old herself.

She looked like my kind of dog, so, no owner being forth-coming, I adopted her. Rested, treated and fed, she was beautiful - a large, heavy-boned brindle beauty - a Malamute/Shepherd cross, perhaps.

"I'll try sledding with her this fall," I thought. *"She's the perfect type and can replace my old Malamute."* Loup's wolfish appearance never failed to impress me - she was the most beautiful dog!

As often happens to me, the gods were laughing. Beauty is as beauty does - and Loup? She did nothing! I guess I should have suspected something when, one night the dogs sounded a ferocious "Intruder alert!" The other dogs got up to patrol our perimeters, and Loup? She crawled out of the closet where she always slept and got into bed with me. "Let the other dogs take care of that intruder!"

Perhaps the fact that she lies down to eat should have foreshadowed her future as a sled dog. That fall, Loup failed "Sled Dog Training 101." She refused to even take the course, refused to run on the team, or even on a leash beside the team. In fact, when left behind by the rest of us, she decided to wait at our vehicle until we returned.

Well, she's about twelve now, and she gets around very well for her age and size. I speculate that, arthritis being caused by wear and tear on the joints, Loup has escaped its ravages, having never, ever really stressed them.

Loup is great with people. Actually, she's more like a LuLu than a Loup. Her thick double coat with its dark brown and black guard coat hides a very light, even blonde undercoat. She greets everyone with a wide grin and friendly interest. Friend or stranger, it's all the same to her.

Her favourite trick is to sit for a treat - no, wait! That's her only trick! And she does look beautiful stretched out on our sofa (all 80 pounds of her), head on a cushion.

It just irks me! She never even tried to pull that sled, never even considered trying. And she's so perfect for it. I guess at twelve, I may as well let it go - all the other sled dogs are long gone and I can't see her changing her mind now. I'm not bitter, though.

You should see her when I ask her, "Loup, who is your favourite person in the whole world?" Head up, eyes sparkling, "I know this one!" attitude, Loup answers in her high-pitched, breathless, "little girl" dog howl, "You! You! You!! You!! You!"

MAN'S BEST FRIENDS

When I got up the other morning, I couldn't help but smile. Our young Border Collie, Hogan, gave a long, luxurious stretch and a very wide, loud, multi-toned yawn - aoa-yooo-gra-graa-ha! Then, with sparkling eyes and a wagging tail, he started his day.

Later, in the Wal-Mart parking lot, a smiling passerby pointed out a large, very full SUV. We both looked into its partially-opened windows and counted a black and white dog and two Siberian Huskies seated in the driver's seat, two Siberians in the passenger's seat and four, maybe five Sibes in the back. As we met their blue (and some brown) eyes we grinned delightedly, and were rewarded by friendly eyes and wagging tails when I asked, "How are you guys?" I was still smiling as I walked into the store, quite taken by their friendly demeanor and their quiet, accepting greetings. I smiled again as I thought, "Someone is in for a tussle if they want to sit in that driver's seat!"

Then, at the grocery store, I met an old friend who had recently lost her aged cat. She recounted how, when she had lost her hair from treatment for breast cancer, that cat had changed its long-time sleeping habits - and slept with her body wrapped around my friend's bare head. It was clear that she was affected by her cat's thoughtfulness and caring. I thought, "*Heaven must have been missing an angel while that cat was here.*" Smiling, I blinked back tears and swallowed to relieve the lump in my throat.

At the end of that day, when I rose from my chair in the living room to go to bed, I smiled as my five shadows immediately followed. The three who are still able jumped on the bed and settled near me - a head resting on my knee, one on my hip and one on my shoulder. The faithful old ones lay on their soft beds beside mine, wagging their tails as I smiled and told them how good they were.

I drifted off to sleep, a small smile on my face as I thought about how they enhance our lives with their friendship and caring, and how they make us smile.

THE BEATLES AT DUNROAMIN'

Have you heard that DunRoamin' is having an open house at the Florenceville Veterinary Clinic on Saturday? It should be an interesting day, a chance to see old friends and meet new ones, maybe even adopt your very own permanent friend. Our cat and kitten numbers have sky-rocketed over the "unwanted kitten" season and we are very eager to get these little guys into caring homes. We will also have a BBQ, a dessert table, and other interesting attractions, including a teddy bear hospital for the kids.

DunRoamin' is a very unique rescue group. You never know what you will find there. Any shelter will have regular dogs and cats, but at DunRoamin'— well, ours are very special!

Take, for instance, our miniature Eastern cougars. We have the more common brown/brindle ones (check out Jebus) and even the more exotic, rarely glimpsed black miniature cougars

(Rant and Rave). Their miniature size makes them less dangerous and much more easily handled than their full-sized counterparts. Enjoy being the owner of interesting, unique animals. The vets here will verify that they are one of a kind!

We also have cat-zillas! They are cranky and cross and more than ready for forever homes! Could you love the beautiful Lolita? She is a gorgeous beauty queen and is slightly temperamental. Are you up for a challenge?

We have many Desperate Housecats and dogs, too. Could you love us for our whole lives? We are not disposable! But we're cute, we're cuddly and some of us are just a little bit catty! We also have "Fat Cat" adoptions. Check out our Peabody! Adopt a beautiful plus-size cat. More love purr pound! Or, adopt a Fat Cat Wannabe - make it a "do-it-yourself" project! Our Fat Cats double as a comforter – all of our pets do!

Try "Cat Fax." We have certified, pre-owned cats, many makes and models. Standard four-paw drive, multi-point inspection, better than new— all spayed and neutered, vaccinated, medically checked, nails trimmed. Ask for "Cat Fax" history!

Do you like bugs? You don't usually find them on the adoption list at a rescue - but ours are different, they are special. We have The Beatles - John, Paul, George and Ringo! They're growing well, the little slugs, even though they have been hand-raised (and they are not as grubby as they were when they arrived). In fact, they are fat as June bugs, and starting to crawl all over our nursery.

It seems to me that their attitudes say *Got To Get You Into My Life*. They try to *Act Naturally*, but when *All You Need Is Love*, it's hard to see them *In a World Without Love*. They don't need a *Day Tripper*, they want homes for *Eight Days A Week*. Oh, they're not desperate, they're not shouting *Help, I Need Somebody*! Not yet! They're still teaching each other to be kittens. Still, *It Won't Be Long* before *It's All Too Much*, and we can't just *Let It Be*. *We're Searchin'*, we want to send them to loving homes, saying *Take Good Care Of My Baby* as they start down *The Long And Winding Road,* singing in purrfect harmony, *Til There Was You* and *To Know Her is to* Love *Her* and will you still love me *When I'm Sixty Four*. They'll say they got by as neonatal kittens *With A Little Help From My Friends*. That was *Yesterday,* now they want to *Come Together* and they know *One and One Is Two*. That's what they want - to be one of two friends.

So, will you come to our open house, or will you leave us *Crying, Waiting, Hoping?*

I could go on, but this is getting long and I'm not a *Paperback Writer*, so this is *The End*.

AVA

It seems to be happening all too frequently. That it would happen at all is unbelievable. Yet, another tiny kitten has been brought to DunRoamin', the victim of a horrific act. She had to have been thrown from a car. That's the only way that this complex of injuries has been seen to occur at DunRoamin'.

This victim was even tinier than the previous two victims, at less than eight weeks of age. With great bravery and stoicism, she has borne the pain and necessary treatment and surgery to repair her little face and reattach her tiny nose. Despite the pain and swelling, despite the overnight cold, despite her malnutrition, her dehydration and her horrible flea burden, she was *not* ready to die. She plans to *live* to be a very old cat! And she has shown more character, more love and caring and way more sensitivity than the crass and cruel people who perpetrated this act against her.

Tiny Ava was brought to DunRoamin' and has finally finished her treatments, allowing her to be adopted into an excellent home. This tiny favourite, despite her rough start, never failed to purr and knead to thank her caregivers for their attention. She brought "sweet" to a whole new level, and "cute"! Well, we've never seen the like. She's okay now, as we say, but it hurts to think that someone out there deliberately caused this pain and suffering, inflicted it on this tiny scrap of catdom. For what reason? I don't want to understand how people can do this! I wish they could see the suffering they have caused, the needless pain they have inflicted on this tiny baby.

Ava endeared herself to all her caregivers. In fact, she endeared herself to everyone and, healed and healthy, she was finally able to move into her forever home with her new family. Happy ending!

THE PAIN OF CHAINS

She's been miserable for years—at least three— since she was a mere puppy. She's existed in circumstances alien to her species - alone, trapped, chained and hungry, thirsty and forlorn, not allowed to run, hardly acknowledged. Her name was Sally, not that anyone ever used it.

Her coat was straw-like, dry and brittle, over protruding hipbones, visible ribs, a painfully arched back and a stiff, painful neck. No one had cared about her in a long time. She was rarely fed, always thirsty. Her body condition, her coat and her hopeless demeanour were mute testimony to her hellish life.

Her eyes watched fearfully as she was approached. Would that person jar her neck? Would the sharp pains get worse?

To her amazement, the huge heavy chain was removed, a gentle hand patted her head, and a lovely lady removed her from the small area in which she had lived for her entire life - restrained by that hateful, painful chain. Her steps were hesitant and stiff. Her neck hurt so badly, injured and traumatized by the unrelenting drag of that heavy chain. What was happening?

Her well-fed owner carelessly gave her to the lovely lady who immediately took her for medical care. She wanted to explore the car, gaze in amazement at the big world, explore the hospital, but the pain in her neck came back forcefully when she moved her head. She held her head very still while her eyes roamed over this big new world. She had not seen anything but her narrow prison for so long.

She had felt invisible! Couldn't anyone see how she was trapped, how she had no life? Almost no food? No love? Year after endless year, she had baked in the sun, frozen in the snow, fought flies and mosquitoes and quivered in fear at the approach of wild animals - coyotes, bobcats, bear. She knew she could not escape. She had already tried, many times. She knew that someday her captors would look out their window and she would be dead - probably dead for several days before they noticed. It was the only escape she could envision.

Why couldn't people see her? Why did no one help her? There were neighbours nearby. Couldn't they see her? Maybe she really was invisible.

Then came the lovely lady and the lovely ladies at the rescue place, and the medicine to take the pain away, and food, and a bath. She couldn't remember ever feeling this good, not since she lived with her mother. She felt safe, she felt ... *visible*! She was comforted, petted. She had a soft bed, and food. She had company!

She felt her tail wag. Her stiff neck would not allow her to see it, but she was sure it was wagging. "*When was the last time,*" she thought, "*that my tail wagged for joy?*" She couldn't remember!

"Let's call her Landon!" someone said. "*I like it!*" she thought. '*Landon' sounds like she is important to someone! They say I'll find a new home! If I do, it will be the first 'home' that I've ever had! I really want a 'home!'"*

Is there a Sally (or a Sully) in your neighbourhood? Is that dog "invisible," too? Don't let them be invisible. Make a statement: "Chained dogs will not be tolerated!" Nor will neglect and abuse!

LANDON

For those of you who regularly follow our DunRoamin' articles, you'll remember that last week we told you about our newest patient, Landon. She had been rescued from a terrible life - tied with a heavy chain that damaged and caused pain in the muscles in her neck and back, with little food, water or shelter. Shortly after her arrival at DunRoamin', one of our strongest supporters volunteered to foster her, even though she currently has six cats and a dog of her own.

Landon's physical injuries will take a while to heal, but she seems to be doing much better, now that she's finally experienced love, compassion, concern, medical care, a full belly, lots of fresh water and absolute safety. It's a first for her, even though she's at least three years old. She's extremely grateful to have a life again. In fact, she has written home already.

> Dear wonderful vet lady – (she means Dr Monteith)

Thank you so much for taking care of me last week. I know you care about me 'cause you are helping me and making me know that I really am visible.

My foster mudder read the article today about me and felt that I should write you a letter. I agreed with her.

I'm still having a hard time moving my neck but I think it's getting better. My foster mudder massages it for me and then hugs me and gives me a kiss and tells me I'm a wonderful girl and so deserving of love and attention. Why didn't my former slave owners feel that way about me? I was with them for so much longer. Why couldn't they see what they were doing to me?

Anyway, that's the past and I'm going to live for and look forward to the future. I know I won't be able to stay where I am permanently, but I also know that until I find a forever home I can stay here. I like it here. I get to sleep on the couch, on nice cushions and on blankets on the floor . . . wherever I want to, actually. And my water and food bowls never go empty.

The first few times she took me outside, I thought she was going to chain me up. So I went to a place where I'd at least have some shelter if she did. But she didn't! She coaxed me out from under the steps and took me back inside. I've never been inside so much in my life!! I really really like it.

Anyway, I think it's time for another nap. I'm taking a lot of those too. I don't have to worry about some wild animal or human coming to hurt me, so I can relax.

Happy to be able to write,

- Landon

TAKING A BITE OUT OF LIFE

When someone commented that maybe I'd "bitten off more than I could chew" this time, I looked at the bruises on my forearms, right index finger and right ankle and thought *"I'm not the one who is biting."*

And I wasn't. It was Hugh! Found wandering the streets, encased in a thick helmet of matted fur, much like a turtle's shell, the little cocker mix was initially taken to the shelter where his terrible mats were removed. Despite feeling more comfortable, he was still angry and aggressive. He bit staff there several times until he was deemed unlikely to get adopted and booked to be put down for his aggression. The little guy meant business, was hyper-alert and ready for trouble. That's why we gave him the name Hugh - after Shannon's first boss - and we gave him one month to change his ways.

The first couple of days with me were confrontational, even for a hard-bitten old dog person like myself. It seemed that Hugh's answer to everything was to turn and bite. Such common behaviours as holding him by the collar, gently encouraging him to go outside with a foot pushing his rear, assisting him into a crate, touching his tail, his feet or his ears or moving one's hand quickly towards him - all resulted in attempts to bite.

And yet, cooing gently to him, I could roll him on his back, remove food from his jaws and pull burrs from his coat. While extremely wary and alert for danger, his eyes did not have the hardened viciousness of a dog that truly wishes to damage. My impression was that of a young dog wary of abuse. Instead of walking out the door he darted out, looking over his shoulder. It was evident that he loved being touched and he would practically purr while having his head patted, but when it was time to leave my lap he would snap at my hands.

"Fear and self-defence", I thought, *"That's why he's biting. Also lack of confidence"* So, we started remedial training.

"Hugh", I said, ignoring the growls, "Come with me!" Each growl was ignored or met with my "Aahh!" But each accepting move was met with praise, rewards and more petting. Hugh was no time in figuring out that, here, biting was not necessary, and that cuddling is good!

His month is up now and, you guessed it. I'm in love. His real personality is shining through and he's a fun, feisty little guy who plays with the big dogs until he's exhausted, then cuddles with whomever is available.

He stayed with friends last week while I was away and, I'm very proud to say that there were no biting incidents, not even any attempts. He went to town and met a new friend who cuddled him with not so much as a faint threat.

Hugh loves the car now, confidently visits new friends, can be scooped onto your lap, scooted out the door and can have his feet, ears and tail touched and gently pulled without considering the need to draw blood.

I'm so proud! He's come a long way, and so easily! He wants to be a good dog. He wants to trust. He wants to be with people, despite his abusive past. I think he could live in the right family as the perfect little companion now, except for one thing that I discovered today: Hugh chews shoes! We'll work on that, too.

KITTENS, KITTENS, KITTENS

It's like that annoying Justin Bieber song at DunRoamin' when I go into the kitten room: I'm like, baby baby baby, ooh, baby baby baby, ooh, baby baby baby . . . They are everywhere, well over a dozen of them - most too young to be away from their mothers, but struggling to survive without them, nonetheless. The DunRoamin' kitten room is filled to capacity. Babies are curled up in little cat houses, on blankets, in the litter box, on stools, in their food dishes, on soft towels, meowing for attention, climbing up our legs, trying to groom themselves, and . . . don't sit down! It's like a thousand tiny acupuncture needles walking up your legs and arms, across your neck and up your face - they just want the comfort of closeness, but they keep sliding off!

Their demands are simple - feed me, cuddle me, pick me up, save me! They miss the attention of their mothers. They are missing a normal, natural upbringing, being raised the way nature intended. They are missing a nurturing mother who teaches them cat secrets, secrets of which we foster mothers are oblivious. How can we raise them properly if we don't know the secrets? We can only try, doing our best, wishing that the owners had spayed their animals.

You know, when I see these little guys year after year, abused, neglected, starving, abandoned, parasitized, I think how great it is that the majority of pet owners spay and neuter their animals. It's easy to spay cats at five or six months of age, before they start churning out litter after unwanted litter.

Volunteers have been losing a lot of sleep, feeding the littlest ones every two or three hours, day and night, from tiny little bottles, trying to give them a good start, trying to keep them alive. They are here and they need help, but -- if they had not been conceived, their parents had not been allowed to breed, many people would rest easier without the knowledge of the suffering these kittens have already experienced. And - where are their mothers? They didn't abandon their kittens in cardboard boxes in the ditches.

It's no secret that two intact cats and the offspring of their offspring can, over seven years, (even factoring in the extreme kitten mortality rates and the young/adult deaths in cats living like this) still result in four hundred surviving, potentially breeding cats - cats who had nowhere to go long before their grandparents were born.

In tribute to those responsible pet owners, I propose a new DunRoamin event - the Spay Pride Parade! We would set up a mardi gras-like event with food kiosks, education booths, beer gardens and lots of music. Our spayed queens and neutered toms would be present marching in front of the clinic where many of the DunRoamin cats are living, to discuss their chosen alternative lifestyles and to encourage everyone to avoid litters. I think it could work!

By the way - what would you do if you could have eighteen children a year? .... Exactly! Please spay and neuter!

BABY MIKEY

The tiny kitten, "Baby Mikey" died in his fourth week of life. He was found the previous day in a precarious situation, severely injured by trauma, neglected and abandoned. Dumped in the grocery store parking lot, he was thin, covered with fleas, and worse – the upper half of his right hind leg was broken. Under his long grey hair was the tiniest, most fragile of bodies.

He was "between a rock and a hard place", medically speaking. None of our medications could safely or effectively alleviate his pain. The leg needed to be stabilized. The bone ends were visible. And yet, he was so young, so tiny, so damaged. Was he strong enough to attempt the anaesthetic?

If whoever dropped him there had just given him two more weeks with his mother, time to grow and gain strength, he may have been able to survive. If they had just been compassionate and spayed his mother, or, failing that, provided him with the care and safety that was his due…

Forced to attempt treatment for all his injuries, attempt to control his pain and prevent him from succumbing to those injuries, we carefully administered anaesthesia and surgically repaired all that was possible, carefully suturing his fragile, thin skin together.

Baby Mikey woke up! Later, to our relief, he managed to eat - and wanted more. We dared to start hoping. Several hours later, he began having breathing problems and, despite our attempts to intervene, he expired. We were devastated! Holding his tiny body in one hand, part of me wished that he had never been born, never suffered like he did, never glimpsed life - only to die, tossed away like a piece of garbage.

As I look around DunRoamin' part of me wishes most of our wards had never been born. There is just no need of adding more unwanted kittens to the huge numbers of unwanted cats!

Oh, I don't object to kittens – there's nothing more adorable! But, until this world has something more to offer them than short lives filled with suffering, or humane deaths at over-filled animal shelters – I object to litter after litter from breeding pets. I object to the "Yup, the cat went out and got herself pregnant again" mentality. (Here's a newsflash for you – you let her get pregnant and you are responsible for her!)

I object to the "throw away pet" attitude and I object to the lack of caring for these tiny innocent beings.

But - I can object until the cows come home and it won't make a difference. Only you – can make a difference.

Baby Mikey, innocent, struggling, pain-wracked, parasitized, flea-ridden, lost and alone – died in his fourth week of life. I object. DunRoamin' objects. Please object. Please spay and neuter.

OAKLEY

When I bring a new dog home to the house for fostering, my dogs react predictably.

Mick, the old collie mix, completely ignores the newcomer – does not even deem to shift his gaze in that direction. Seven, the nine-year old Siberian Husky, swoops down on the new dog, male or female, her eyes hard, expression saying, "I'm the top dog here!!" and proceeds to read all she can from the intimidated new arrival. Miles, the Border Collie mix and acknowledged playground bully, does his usual shove, followed by a thorough body search. The young Border Collie, Hogan, all sweetness and light, engages his new friend with a ball and a welcoming smile. Jerry, the young German Shepherd, says "Hello!" and makes a hurried but neutral inspection, no doubt remembering the not-too-distant past when he was in the newcomers hot seat. Little Hughie, the small (by our standards) cocker mix boldly enters the pack, a

"Don't mess with me!" expression on his face, "I'll take on all comers!" attitude explicit in his short stride. He has the classic "little man" or Napoleon complex and he all but sputters as he assesses his new rival for signs of weakness.

It's a good show all around. I observe but say nothing, since I know, as do the dogs, that it is not Seven who is the top... dog here. That's why I was so surprised at their reaction when we brought Oakley into the house the night she was found shot, dehydrated and limping on three legs. She was exhausted, the picture of defeat.

In a previously unprecedented move, Mick stood, walked to her side, sniffed noses with her and wagged his tail before walking away. Seven approached rapidly, head and tail up, but stopped, sniffed noses, dropped her head and tail and left Oakley in peace. Miles merely acknowledged her with a brief sniff before moving away. Hogan gently licked her face in a promise of friendship, and Jerry and Hugh greeted her with very unusual restraint.

In no time, our dogs were lying down, watching Oakley, but not challenging or stressing her.

"Is this what I think it is?" we asked ourselves. "Are they leaving her in peace because they are aware of her injuries and weakened state? Are they showing compassion, empathy even?"

It seemed to require all of Oakley's effort just to stand. The dogs appeared to accept that she was weak and needed help.

Wait a minute! Were the dogs showing humanity? Did the "animal" behaviour originate from humans? How could this be? Who was showing kindness and compassion?

You know, I once heard a story about a Lab who accidentally shot a duck hunter by jumping on his gun. Come to think of it, that's the only time I can recall when an animal has shot a person. Something to think about, isn't it?

WHO'S HUGH?

You know, there's something to be said for average intelligence and a calm settled demeanor. I spent a very pleasant Saturday at the DunRoamin' booth at Florenceville-Bristol's Buttermilk Creek Days, the summer festival and craft sale. I was accompanied by Jerry, DunRoamin's young German Shepherd rescue dog. He was perfect - gentlemanly, restful, friendly but not too friendly. He greeted and communed with many - children and adults alike, with his laid-back, relaxed attitude. He was dignified but approachable. Occasionally he revealed his lighter, fun side by coveting a decorative ball on one craft table and by coaxing belly rubs from some of his more gullible new friends. He was a delight! Such a great dog - and he's like that at home. If I settle into a chair with a book, he's happy to lie on the sofa and nap. If I go out to play ball, he's a blur - fastest dog in the pack, focussed, athletic. It's all about the ball - get it and bring it to the foster-mudder. He's so great. I love him!

Contrast that with another of my favourite dogs, Hogan, the young Border collie. He's *wound!* There's nothing calm or restful about him! He's all about doing something. He has a ball game in the morning, returns to the house, sides heaving, and before he has his breath back, he's anxiously waiting to go for a walk, then wants a training session (I'm teaching him to dance) and then angles for a drive in the car. Then he harasses the other dogs, teases the pup and bugs Jerry until poor Jer climbs into my lap to escape him, and then - well, then he wants to go out for another training session. He stares at me from across the room until the hairs stand up on my neck. His expression is a curious mixture of pleading, self-pity and accusation. I think, "Bite me, Hogan! You've had plenty of attention for today!" His stare is insistent, his eyes begging "Just one more dance session?"

The other dogs want me to take him out too, so they can sleep in peace, so he'll stop dropping toys on them. Hugh, the cocky little cocker mix has repeatedly threatened to kill Hogan to get some peace. Aware that I would not condone this, Hugh is hiding in his crate to avoid the toys. I can tell, though, from Hugh's stiff body language and steely gaze, that his hold on his temper is tenuous at best. He's fed up with Hogan's constant activity. I totally get that, too! Everyone but Hogan has called it quits for the day. So have I, but I cave under the uncompromising pressure of that constant stare and take Hogie out for a quick run-through of our limited dance routine. I am acutely aware that I am the limiting factor, that it is I who will keep us from So You Think You Can Dance Canada. Yes, he has two left feet, but I have no talent for dancing. He seems to have it all - the brains, the beauty, the energy! Maybe I should be teaching him to do housework and vacuum up dog hairs. I bet he could do it, if I could find a way to teach him. Maybe I'll just buy him a herd of sheep but then -- the poor sheep!

Such great dogs, so different! Then there's the Husky, and how she can escape from anything. And Hugh - we won't go there! This shows how breed can make such a big difference in your relationship with your dog. Research the breed you are interested in, find out what they need before you adopt them. Make sure that you can meet their needs - you may get more than you bargained for!

LESSONS WE HAVE LEARNED FROM OUR STRAYS

In dealing with the local cast-offs and throw-away animals, we at DunRoamin' have learned a lot, both professionally and personally. Dr. Monteith and I have been forced to become thinkers "outside of the box" in dealing with some of the situations that we have faced. We have been forced to use creative thinking to overcome even such small problems as how to accommodate our sick and injured friends. Other grave injuries and illnesses have forced us to grow professionally (often in giant leaps) to deal with obscure and unlikely conditions.

A recent difficult challenge was what to do with thirteen very sick, starving, parasitized and abandoned cats (the Dirty Dozen) late in the evening. How do we treat, medicate, feed, record and accommodate all these sick animals, set up treatment plans for their severe disease with the horrific complications, and then arrive at work in the morning, smiling, ready for a full day and a week of round the clock on-call for emergencies? Fortunately for me, the smiling stuff fell on Dr. Monteith's shoulders. Those guys taught us a lot about triage, severe eye disease, and respiratory disease. They also taught us about ourselves and challenged our commitment. I like to think that we passed the challenge.

More than that, though, these cats and others have individually helped us to learn many life lessons. They have exemplified them. For instance: The Dirty Dozen - if you could see them now, active, happy, playing. They are happy to be alive and not ashamed to show it. One little guy, Jaden, is such a delight! Although he cannot see from one eye, his other eye is scarred and his head is permanently tilted to the right affecting his balance, he is the "Kitten from Hell!" He's up your pant leg, leaping to the cat tree, rolling on the floor with his newest victim. He's a terror, and a personal favourite. He loves to cuddle, to play, to eat, to visit and to sleep in the kitten pile. He's happy with what he has and what he can do, and that is: get into more stuff and more trouble than any of the other cats. He loves life. He's okay now.

Then there's Tibby, the young cat who determinedly walked on her knees when the lower bones (the tibias) in both her back legs were broken. She is a fighter. Nothing could stop her and we were proud to be able to help her with her broken bones. She too, is okay now, but she would be more okay if she had that permanent home, the one where she was loved and coddled and didn't have to compete with thirty other cats. Oh, she's not complaining, I, sort of, am, because I want to see her where she belongs and in a home that she deserves.

Until Each One Has a Home

From the beautiful, snow white, lovely but volatile Lolita, we all learned why female cats are called "Queens" - a lesson we won't soon forget!

From Hugh, the biting little cocker mix, we learned that it is important to stand up for yourself, but that when things are on the upswing, it is time to forgive and - well, if not forget, at least change your approach. It's the only way to get bacon treats!

Dwhite, the filthy, flea-ridden white street cat, has shown us, again, not to judge a book by its cover, that looks can be deceiving, and that just because he is a street person, does not mean he is not worthy of respect. Under that grimy exterior, to my delight, lies a personality of pure gold, a perfect gentleman - loving, kind, and friendly to all. With the use of our facilities, Dwhite "cleaned up real good" and now even looks the part.

I think tiny baby Cordelia's heroic struggle with abandonment, parasitism and disease is one of the bravest stories. She has fought courageously— at first, just for her next breath, then, for more food, and then to regain her strength. In the last few days she has fought a winning battle with her tangled, stained coat, mercilessly taking control of every wayward hair until now, finally and at last, she looks like the six week old kitten that she is. She showed us that body size is no indicator of the size of one's will, one's strength, and one's perseverance. Amazing character comes in many packages. Cordelia is my little hero!

From Hogan, the young Border collie, we learned to call the ball the "Thing," rather than spell B-A-L-L. Border collies can spell, you know! And, from tiny Helen, the worst of the

Dirty Dozen, who has lost vision in both eyes due to her terrible infection, we have learned to make the best of what you have, much like her brother, Jaden. Helen runs and plays in the warm room that she knows so well, playing like a crazy kitten, wrestling with her roommates and batting at her toys. Yes, it is horrific that she has lost both eyes to preventable disease - but she's alive and she's enjoying life and living it well.

All of our animals seem to have the right idea, the best way of coping. They seem to have a matter-of-fact approach. It happened, it's behind us, now let's get on with life. I think they will, too, once they get that home meant for them, the one where they are accepted as they are and as they have accepted life. I hope those homes come soon for them.

LET'S ALL BE DUNROAMIN'

In answering the DunRoamin' phone line, lately I've been getting many calls regarding cats or kittens on the street. Well-intentioned callers are asking DunRoamin' to take these cats. We'd love to! BUT - we do not have a building in which to house them, nor do we have staff to attend to all the healthy, but homeless cats out there.

DunRoamin's mandate is to help those whose lives would be lost without veterinary care, without round-the-clock nursing and observation. That is what we do. DunRoamin' vets donate their time and professional services. Veterinary technicians donate their time and skills. Volunteers donate their unique skills to keep DunRoamin' afloat.

Many homeless street cats do not need veterinary intervention (other than the usual worm and flea treatments, and preventative vaccines). Concerned people can and should bring these guys indoors - they very likely will not survive the winter without help. The shelters, if not overcrowded, may be able to help. All one cold little kitty needs from people is a warm room, food, water, and a litter box. That's all. And that will likely save a life, and it certainly will prevent undue suffering.

Then, having prevented the suffering, the cat can live in safety and warmth while you work on other aspects of its care - spaying and neutering, health care. By calling shelters, DunRoamin', Cat Rescue Maritimes, or asking friends and relatives for donations, you can ease the personal cost of these necessary health-care items, and then work on finding permanent homes. You can do it yourself - many people do. Your reward will be in knowing that you have prevented the suffering, cold and starvation to which street cats succumb. You will have prevented litters, therefore decreasing the numbers of street cats. You will have made a pre-emptive strike against perpetuating the unwanted cats on the street, and you will have the unparalleled satisfaction of having helped not one, but potentially many future families. You will have made a difference.

"But I can't ask people to do that," you might think. Why not? Pet overpopulation is a societal problem and will take a responsible society to alleviate it. DunRoamin' supporters do it every day. We ask total strangers, businesses, clients, friends, family and acquaintances to help at every opportunity, every day!

We donate our weekends, our money, and our homes to the support of these little guys. We're asking you to donate, too.

You can help in many ways. Spay and neuter all your own animals. Adopt from shelters, and rescue organizations. Counsel friends and family to spay and neuter, to respect animals and to care for them properly.

Outspoken people and public opinion can change beliefs and attitudes. Let's work on it! Let's become a community that treats others with care and respect - friends, family, neighbours, pets and strays of **all** kinds. Let's cause everyone to be DunRoamin'.

LINK

In the early seventeen hundreds, the English philosopher, Jeremy Bentham, said regarding animal rights, "The question is not 'Can they reason?' nor 'Can they talk?', but 'Can they suffer?" The answer is a resounding *"Yes"*, they can - and they do!

After fourteen years as a nurse in intensive care units and in the ER, I am familiar with the face of suffering. I easily recognize it in the demeanor, in the body language, in the facial expressions and in the eyes of suffering people. When I became a veterinarian, I found the same expressions of suffering in my new set of patients. They were easily recognizable, frighteningly obvious and very, very familiar. I saw that the appearance of suffering transcends species - it looks very much the same. This is not surprising, given that we all have virtually the same central nervous systems (oh, I know that humans have bigger brains - at least some do!) We have the same types of pain receptors, the same synapses carrying messages to our brains, and the same basic needs for life. This is hard to refute, given that the basis for most of our medical advances have come from studies on animals - same physical setup!

So - why do people find it so implausible that pets feel the same pain, cold, hunger, boredom, and loneliness that we would feel in a similar situation? Or - should I ask - why don't some people care that they feel these things?

I'd like to introduce a long-time sufferer - Link. He's DunRoamin's latest poster-boy for suffering. Found wandering near the Beardsley Road in Woodstock, Link had finally broken free of his restraints - sort of. With his age estimated at sixteen to twenty-four months, it is not unreasonable to assume that someone looped a heavy chain (one with which a car could be towed) around the neck of a much smaller Link, and left it that way, without adjusting for the pup's growth. When he was discovered last week dragging several feet of chain down the highway, his rescuers were horrified.

I warn you that this description is graphic, but real life was much worse! The heavy chain was embedded by over two inches into the flesh of Link's neck, the wound an appalling four inches wide and about three inches deep, grossly infected, with finger-like projections of flesh growing though the center of the links - his body's attempt to repair the ongoing damage and constriction of the tight chain. This did not happen overnight or even over weeks. This happened over months - probably eight to ten months! Pretty hard to miss that wound on your dog, or the odour, or the pus running down his neck. Those signs of suffering, too, would have been extremely evident.

After surgically removing the offending chain, cleaning the badly-infected wound and starting the process of closing such a huge wound, Link's vet started large doses of antibiotics for the infection and large doses of analgesia for his pain. His recovery will take weeks. This dog suffered for months. This dog saved himself! Where were his owners? Their visitors? The neighbours? Family? Friends? Why didn't anyone see his predicament? That animals, our pets, can suffer the torture of the damned under our very noses, without one caring person looking out for their well being, or reporting such vile neglect is disgraceful. It should never happen. We know better. We all do. There is no excuse. And, we owe Link. If anyone recognises this dog - this great, gentle, playful, very, very loving dog, who found out this weekend that he can run like the wind and play with other dogs, free of the torturous pull of that heavy chain, if you recognize this lovely guy who just wants to sit at my feet, so he can touch me, you owe it to Link to call the SPCA and report his abuser. Someone must be held accountable for his torture. Someone knows better and must come to terms with this thing that they have done. Chaining dogs is not acceptable - in Link's case, it was criminal!

My friends have tried to calm me by saying "What goes around, comes around." For Link's previous owner's sake, I hope that is not true!

TEACH THEM!

Today I was told about a nine-month-old mixed breed dog (whose mix included Pitbull and Shar pei) who will likely be killed because he has bitten - twice! He has also used the house as a bathroom, barked incessantly and destroyed belongings. His life is in danger. He may not see his first birthday.

He started his life as all dogs do - cute, cuddly, innocent, ready to learn, anxious to please, wanting to bond with that person, his leader - wanting to be that person's best friend. But that person, the one who took that innocent puppy, did not fulfill his obligations to the dog. In adopting him, the new owner became responsible for him and for his welfare - physically, mentally, and emotionally. That person was responsible for feeding, exercising, sheltering and training his new friend. He was responsible for assuring that *his* dog could function as a pet in today's society. We all have that responsibility to our dogs. To say that the dog must be killed when no one has taken the time to teach the pup manners is similar to locking up (or killing) a child who bites. Both need to be taught appropriate manners. Owners of any dog need to teach them acceptable behaviours. "But he won't", I often hear. Yes, he will! If you can't teach him the behaviours he needs, rest assured that someone else can!

First-time dog owners need to find help from trainers in order to train their dogs and to understand how their body language affects what they think they are saying to their dog. You didn't learn to drive a car, read, write or use a computer without some instruction, did you? Logic then dictates that most people don't automatically know how to train dogs or to read their dog's body language.

Most dogs, whose owners try to train them, will learn what it is that the owners want them to do, no matter how confusing the signals and body language of their owners may be. And most dogs, will do what they have been "taught" to do just to please their bumbling owner. That's all it takes, usually: love and good intentions! No beatings!

But some people who arrogantly and carelessly acquire tough, strong working dogs and fail to supply exercise and training - that's just wrong! That sets the dog up for failure.

And, who pays for that failed relationship? The dog! The dog always pays— and often with his life. In times when information is more freely available than ever before, when even small towns like ours have obedience classes, when you can actually take obedience classes on the internet, how can it always be the dog's fault that he doesn't do as wished. How can people be so self-centered and uncaring as to allow their "best friend" to be killed for doing something that he didn't even know was wrong— that his owner didn't teach him was wrong?

We have a lot to answer for when we look at how some of our "best friends" are treated. And I hope that young person "man's up" as they say, and saves his pup's life!

Feral at DunRoamin'

" 'Twas warm there at DunRoamin'
At a cold time of the year.
We're all warm and well-fed,
They say there's naught to fear.

So, if this is really safety
That most here have never known
Before we all relax too much,
I'd rather we were shown.

I'd really like to trust them,
But I've never seen "safe's" face
It seems to mean one thing for us
And one for the human race!

Until Each One Has a Home

So, just because you say so,
Doesn't make it true.
Maybe you can be trusted,
But still, I don't know you! "

She sat there in the cat room,
And didn't move a hair.
She wondered, "*Will he trust me?*"
And tried hard not to care.

She knew he'd find a place to live,
Of that she had no doubt.
He'd either tame and live indoors
Or not, and live life out.

She really wanted him to see
Her interests were his own.
She wanted him to live his life,
In safety, in a home.

He stayed safely at a distance,
He couldn't take a chance.
He watched the others on her lap
And rubbing on her pants.

He didn't know the moment
When he saw his decision made
But he slowly crept up closer,
A compulsion he obeyed

Mildred A. Drost DVM

See, he wasn't born a feral cat
As a kitten, he was a pet,
But they moved away and left him
On purpose, or did they forget?

He'd spent the winter freezing,
And starving and in pain
He thought he'd never ever trust
And go through that again.

But as she slowly reached toward him
And gently stroked his head
She wiped a big tear from her eye
And turned to him and said

"I have no right to ask it,
But I know the life you've led,
If you'll only let me help you
You can be a pet instead."

'Cause that was where he'd started.
He'd really loved his home
He hadn't learned to live outside.
He didn't want to roam.

So he accepted her attention
Became trusting - was her friend!
She showed him just what safety meant -
They're together - till the end.

I AM A DUNROAMIN' VOLUNTEER

DunRoamin' would not be able to function if not for our volunteers - those who fundraise, look after animals and make crafts and toys for sale. One area that uses up many volunteer hours is the cat area in the basement which houses cats who have not yet found permanent or foster homes. It is usually quite full. Our volunteers wear many hats in that job - all of which are very necessary. This is for our volunteers - with many thanks.

I am a DunRoamin' volunteer. I do this on purpose - for free, without being coerced, on my own time. I do it for them - the basement cats, their families and friends. I do it for "the four-legged folk."

I clean and feed the cats at DunRoamin'. I medicate those who need it. I trim nails if necessary. When I feed, I note that each occupant shows interest in and enjoyment of my food offerings. I then stoop and scoop a myriad of litter boxes.

Worse, I note the type, colour and consistency of that which I scoop and report aberrations to the staff, identifying, if possible, the perpetrator of the act. I also note the liquid contributions to these same litter boxes, alert for those which are too small or, more frightening, too large, or even too empty. I eagerly report these changes too

I wash and digitally remove secretions from the eyes and noses of tiny, bony little beings and cheer them on in their first attempts to purr or play. I have occasionally been known to force life-saving food into the mouths of tiny kittens who are so stuffed up that they cannot smell the food. I hug cold, smelly, flea-ridden abscessed cats close to my body for warmth and comfort, knowing full-well that some stains just won't wash out.

I am a scratching post, a warm lap, a chew toy, a safe haven, a loving pat, a kitten catcher, a girlfriend, a referee, a treat provider, a groomer, a scrub woman, a post-op nurse, a foster mother, a transport person, a comforter, a dishwasher, a launderer, and a socializer. I am not prejudiced by size, shape, infirmity, age, colour or breed. I do not prefer stripes, solid colours, splotches, patches or spots. I hug, I wipe, I pick, I play, I clean, I worry and I pray.

When they have all been cared for, I fund-raise so that I may continue with my duties. I council friends, family and strangers on spaying and neutering and on providing good quality of life for their pets. I follow the DunRoamin' website and Facebook page for news of my friends, to see who got a home and to see who got rescued. I have mini celebrations for each event. I check the websites every day, and call other volunteers to check on my friends. I worry.

I am a DunRoamin' volunteer!

Christmas

Doorbell rings, we're all listenin'
In the basement our coats are glistenin'
Will this be the night, will it turn out all right,
Will I be movin' in a home with my new friend?

Gone away is the blue day,
I'm here to stay, it's a new day
I'll purr a love song, as we go along,
Movin' in a home with my new friend.

In my new house we can build a cat tree
Then pretend that I'm a mountain lion.
You say "Will you hurt me? I'll say "Who me?
I'd miss you way too much if you were dyin'"

Later on, I'll conspire,
As I purr by the fire.

Until Each One Has a Home

I'll live unafraid, My adoption fee's paid
Livin' in a home with my new friend.

In the new house we can build a cat tree.
We'll pretend that I'm a circus clown.
We'll have so much fun up on that cat tree,
I'm hopin' that we both don't knock it down.

Later on, you'll perspire,
As I purr by the fire
We've had such great fun, Our bonding is done,
I'm livin' in a home with my best friend

PUPPY FARM CHRISTMAS

> Christmas at the puppy farm
> Was just another day . . .
> - D.C. Butterfield

Local poet, DC Butterfield's brief but effective poem Puppy Farm Christmas, with its feeling of hopelessness, caused me to think about all the puppies that I see from puppy mills (there are many in our area). I treat them for such problems as hip dysplasia, seizures, breathing difficulties brought about by pinched nostrils and problems with their soft palates and/or wind pipes, kneecap alignment issues, and many other abnormalities that affect the quality of life of these dogs (or cats). Never mind the cost that the unsuspecting owners face trying to make their new family members comfortable.

Then there are the breeding dogs who escape the puppy mills, having been incubators for litter after litter, on almost every heat cycle - their tired little bodies stretched and hanging from constant pregnancies and lactation. These lucky dogs, those who have been discarded by the mills, now must learn so many things, such as the meaning of a gentle pat, the thrill of running free outdoors, the comfort of smooth or carpeted floors versus bare wire crates, the relief of being clean and free of matts, the freedom from the pain of infected teeth, eye infections and skin diseases, the love and companionship of a guardian to whom you are a friend - not a commodity, the crazy sensation of driving in a car with the wind in your face, AND the comfort of having good food and water as you need it.

These are not trappings of a population gone to the dogs -they are simply the rights that should be extended to sentient creatures who have the capacity to suffer and who certainly DO suffer as puppy mill captives.

Not sure you would know a puppy mill if you saw one? Well, your new pup might be from a puppy mill if:

1. there are more than two or three breeds available for sale from the same kennel;

2. you are not allowed to see where the animals live or to meet the parents of the puppy;

3. the owner wants to meet you in the Wal-Mart parking lot for pick-up of your puppy;

4. the breeder has "going out of stock" sales;

5. the dogs don't get to go outside (there is no play area for them);

6. there are stacks of dog-filled crates in the production line;

7. the adults are fearful and unsocialized;

8. you bought your pup at a pet store; and/or

9. you need to "rehabilitate" the dog you just bought before it can be a happy family pet.

Best Friends Animal Society (where the TV show "DogTown" is filmed), has a very thoughtful "Puppies Aren't Products" campaign on now. There is very pertinent information on that site including an information booklet on "Rehabilitating Your Rescued Puppy Mill Dog."

I highly recommend the Best Friends site to any animal person, both as a method of informing yourself regarding animal issues and revelling in the rescues and re-homing that Best Friends is doing. Please check it out at www.bestfriends.org

DAILY REPORT

If you need me, I'll be in the basement in the cat room - probably smoking catnip. No, not the kitten room, the adult cat room. The kittens are too young for that. It's not illegal is it - smoking catnip? I just want that mellow, relaxed feeling that the cats get. I like the way their eyes glaze and they get that "Wuz happ'nin'?" look on their faces. Like they don't care and don't have a care - I want that.

Sergeant Pepper? My newest favourite cat? I don't think he's going to die now. Yes, he has a lonely heart, but he just didn't like the brand of food you were feeding. No, can't guarantee he doesn't have that FIP cat disease. The only way that can be definitively diagnosed is after they die. I thought that he was going to die last weekend. That's why I came in so often to carry him around and let him sleep on my lap. By Sunday, when he started playing with my earrings, I started to think that I might be being used. He just wanted to sit on me and absorb my body heat. Oh, and he *only* wanted to eat the Friskies with the salmon shreds, not the chunks! Cats!

Tiny? He's doing fine. So quiet for such a big black and tan guy. I'm worried that his thyroid gland might not be working. He's a lump - has very little energy and he weighs over a hundred pounds. The boxer mix has been reprimanded by Tiny a few times - guess the old guy doesn't like children who don't use good dog manners. Mort has remembered his manners and is much more respectful of Tiny. So am I!

If I had to guess, I think Mort is the chosen one for that friend who wanted to adopt another dog. His dog didn't like Fred (and Fred was being a grouch) but loved Mort. I'll hear later this week who gets the home. The prospective owners don't want to make any mistakes. Oh, by the way, they may be interested in a cat. They don't have one because their dog teases cats and the cats she knows won't stand up to her. I said that we have the cat for him - Lolita! She will have both dogs trained in seconds. Hope she doesn't hurt them too bad! She'll only have to tell them off once. It worked with me, anyway.

That old Fred is quite a character. He probably started the fight that got him hurt. He didn't deserve to lie in the ditch for that long, though. He has no idea that he's in his teens. In fact, since we started his arthritis medication, I think he feels years younger. He's so funny. Reminds me of those grouchy guys in that movie *Grumpy Old Men*. He'll take on any dog who tries to take what's his. Good thing he can't aim a shotgun. He really is old for a shepherd, but he's not ready to go yet. I think I've found someone who's willing to give him TLC for whatever good time he has left.

The new kitten, the orange one - that's Elton John. He's quite the crooner. The other kitten with him is Encore. She was found in a field by herself when she was tiny. Good thing she had a good set of lungs. Yeah, Elton loves to be touched - he's Lilly-Beth's brother and acts just like her. Encore has been waiting to come in until we had a spot for her. She was being fed well, but is too small to be outside in this weather. She wouldn't survive the winter. Now she just needs some handling to get more tame. She doesn't know it yet, but she wants to be a house cat! Elton just wants to be with people. He'd be great with kids.

The two cats in that kennel? Oh, they're returns. They were adopted a few weeks ago but brought back because they are "no good." Seem quite cuddly and friendly to me. It's better to have them here if they aren't wanted. We'll find them the right home. Oh, and, by the way, the reason it smelled so bad in here today is that Darth, that lazy old tom, can't be bothered burying stuff in his litter box. He's layin' there like, "Take care of that, would ya, and on your way back, bring me another can of wet food." Wouldn't hurt him to clean himself up a bit, either. He'll never get a home looking like that.'

Well, gotta go. Try to keep the numbers down today, would ya?

IS "GOOD ENOUGH" THEN "GOOD ENOUGH" NOW?

Today someone told me about some people who were clubbing little stray kittens to death at a local workplace. As I was dealing with my disgust, I commented that this is a situation better dealt with by the SPCA, not DunRoamin'.

As further discussion ensued, someone said, "Well, what are they supposed to do with the kittens? There are cats everywhere!" My number one answer to that is "Spay and neuter your animals!"

But, to the immediate point, what were they supposed to do? Nowhere in my most hidden thoughts does "pummel and bludgeon those babies to death" occur. I think, "Well, find them homes, take them to a shelter, find a warm barn and continue to feed them, even call DunRoamin' (although we are struggling to accommodate those that we have). But - club kittens to death!?!?

Someone even said, "I watched my grandfather drown kittens when I was a kid. What was wrong with that?" Well, in your grandfather's time, over fifty years ago, it was the best we had to offer, and it was done with reluctance, regret and remorse, but was necessary, given the times, to control barn cat populations. "But," I was told, "if it was good enough then, why not now?"

By that line of reasoning and ignoring the advancements that have been made in the last fifty years, it should be good enough to drive the same farm machinery, grow the same crops, with the same fertilizers and herbicides that were used then. Hay should be brought to barns in the same way our grandfathers did. Houses should be insulated as they were in those times, and wages - they were good enough for our grandfathers! Don't even mention computers. As a society, we have changed markedly, both in our social beliefs and our economic status. Why, then, must we cling to the old ways of dealing with animals? There are more humane and animal rescue groups springing up than ever before. One of the most watched television channels is Animal Planet!

My mind balks at the thought of holding a small creature under water while it struggles desperately for air and for life. They didn't ask to be born. They are here because of us. We owe them a life. And beating a tiny creature to death! I can't fathom that reality - the pain and the fear!

Another thought occurs, too. Ever try to catch a wild animal? I've never even caught a frightened cat, let alone a wild one. Therefore, if these animals are being caught and killed, isn't it possible that they are tame animals? Maybe they were someone's pets?

HILTON

We have a new house guest here on Dog Hill this week. His name is Hilton. While he may not be the cutest pup I've ever seen, he does have many endearing qualities, one of which is his total and complete trust in us and in all the other dogs here.

That means he trusts the ADHD/OCD sufferer, Freeman, who has never been ready for adoption - but he gets a little better each year. Then there's Easy, the Pitbull mix Houdini who was adopted and returned five times; Dreyfus, the huge, hairy mix whose soulful eyes easily scan the kitchen counter tops for delectable tidbits; the once beautiful, now aged and very grouchy Collie mix, Mick; the dog yard bully, Miles; the beautiful husky, Seven (since Hilton's arrival, she's Seven of Nine); the whirling dervish Border Collie, Hogan; and Hilton's favourite, the Shepherd, Jerry.

Hilton is learning the basics from these guys and he's learning fairly quickly. (You know, the things that you do once and then see the error of your ways.) So far, he's solid on several concepts. They include: you don't tug on Freeman's nape, you don't . . . uh . . . pee into the wind, you don't grab food that's Mick's, that's danger! And you don't bite the Pitbull's shin! (We can thank the weather for the "peeing into the wind" thing. The wind is strong up here on the hill.)

Hilton's been learning how to live with us and make friendships. Jerry, the Shepherd, is Hilton's favourite buddy. He's also Hilton's favourite warm spot, his favourite bed, his favourite chew toy, his favourite squeaky toy, and his favourite tug toy. Jerry tolerates the pup's attentions and at times even seems to find some humour in Hilton's antics. He doesn't seem to enjoy being the squeaky toy, though. I'm waiting to see if Jer will stand up for himself someday.

We love watching the two play, but repeatedly I find my mind returning to the big question: what is in Hilton's lineage? Could he be a Collie mix? Maybe some Lab? Some Husky? He was surrendered to us by someone who was told that he was part Shar-pei (don't see it), part Spaniel (nope, don't see that either!), and part Terrier (nope, not a hint). Best guess? Part very mixed breed dog and part mixed breed dog. No specific breed affiliations visible at present. That should make little Hilton a . . . well . . . a mixed mix, I guess.

Still, after knowing the little guy for just over twenty four hours, having allowed him to sleep in my bed and chew on my nose, I think I can say this with some certainty: *this pup has very sharp teeth.* And a great temperament. He'll make someone a great pet and a fine, intelligent companion. That Hilton, he'll be a *good* dog, regardless of what he ends up looking like.

FREEMAN & ME

One might gain the impression from reading these weekly DunRoamin' articles that our animals, once removed from their dire circumstances and adopted into loving homes, would live happily ever after. I like that view of their world, even though it does sound like a fairy tale. Truth be told, our rescued animals are the same as all the others, the same as humans. They have their moments. They have their little quirks, and they get in trouble.

As we say, "I'm only human," and are not perfect, they, too, are only feline or canine, and they, too are not perfect. (Perhaps more perfect than some humans, but I won't go there!)

Of all the animals rescued over years and years of rescues, one animal, a dog named Freeman, has more than adequately demonstrated this observation.

Brought to me by my "friend," Dr. Monteith to "give her a break from him" for "just a few days," Freeman's immediately post-rescue behaviour had been so horrific that, even with both Dr. Monteith and Freeman sedated, she still found his behaviour intolerable.

Somehow it never seemed to be "the right time" to take him back and he was more manageable in our fenced areas and runs. Never aggressive, Freeman was bizarre in his behaviours and even the other dogs couldn't figure him out. Still, with our tolerance for dogs and our experience with training, Freeman has never been "ready to adopt out."

In the intervening six years, while we have worked with him, while waiting for him to be "picked up," Freeman has chewed the block heater cord from my car, eaten five pairs of sandals, seven pairs of shoes, one pair of crocs, and two pairs of boots, including my favourite knee-high black leather dress boots. He has chewed holes in my clothing, and torn and scattered the feathers from two down pillows resulting in a lovely "Charlie Brown" snowfall effect of feathers covering all horizontal surfaces in my bedroom. He has chewed the corners off my bedspread, ripped molding from the hall, left huge bear-like claw marks on my coffee table (while using it as a platform to launch himself to higher elevations in an attempt to retrieve the few breakable ornaments remaining on my living room's highest shelves.) He has assisted in our Yule-tide celebrations by removing all three sets of lights from our outside tree and chewing them into convenient two-foot sections (as well as removing and destroying our grapevine wreath snowman and its decorative holder plus the piece of siding to which it was attached). He has run away and hidden from my obligatory searches in the black-mud swampy area surrounding the village sewage treatment system (how much of that wet land is due to effluent from that system, I wonder?)

He has destroyed more than 200 dog toys and I have lost count of the squeakers he has eaten (and the socks!) He has climbed on our kitchen counter repeatedly, the second our backs were turned, to steal roasts, pies, cookies, doughnuts, and bags of gummie bears, and has somehow succeeded in swallowing each and every prize, without choking, before it can be removed from his gaping maw. He seems incapable of remorse. A quick learner, he can now open the cupboards, the closets, the laundry hamper and the shower (although he hates soap in his eyes and no longer attempts to climb in). His attempts to play have resulted in a myriad of tooth-shaped bruises on my forearms, hands, knees, ankles and feet. No, he would never bite, but his teeth seem to "hit" me a lot.

He has worn out three citronella anti-bark collars, SPCA recommended to deter incessant barking, and the cost of replacement batteries is becoming prohibitive. Still, mosquitoes don't bother him in the summer.

A friend says Freeman gets "a little better every year." After six long years with this guy, (Freeman, I mean) I can't put a label on him or his behaviour, but I do know this: if he lives to be thirteen or fourteen we'll be the grateful recipients of the seniors' pension before we get any real or lasting peace!!

Still, there's that one moment just before I go to bed when Freeby comes to me, sits quietly to be petted and gives his "mudder" a gentle kiss before returning to his assault on the innocent contents of the garbage can, when I think, "He's not so bad . . . he deserves a good life, just like everyone else!!"

We wouldn't give him up for anything. We think Freeman is hilarious and . . . Dr. Monteith - I'm not bitter!

DREYFUS

I should tell you about my newest best friend, Dreyfus. He came to DunRoamin' about two months ago, having lived in an enclosure for the previous two years. He's a large dog, black with a small bit of tan trim. About six inches taller than any of my other dogs, he's a cross between something very big and something very hairy (with a chunk of something very loving thrown in). After twenty-four hours with us, his eyes began to sparkle and that sad worried look started to disappear. He no longer feared being left outside when sent out on business trips. Although two months ago he had no idea what a dog bed was, he now will only sleep on his special dog bed, pacing and whining until I make Jerry move to another, less-favoured bed.

Big as he is, he always seems to think that no one notices him and insists on standing where he cannot be missed - in my personal space, breathing from his opened mouth as I try to relax in my armchair. His face is so close to mine that my glasses alternately fog and unfog with his breathing. His eyes are always locked on mine, not in that compelling, hypnotizing way of the Border collie, Hogan, but in the soft, sweet, gentle and happy way of a lovely dog who is no longer alone and lonely, but comfortable at home, safe and secure with family. I mutter,"I SEE you, Dreyfus," as I strain to see past him to catch the last five minutes of my riveting Law and Order show.

He makes me smile. Last week, he finally got it. That round ball thing - they want you to bring it back. It's sort of, like, a game! And if you give it back, they'll throw it again and you get to run after it again! He's so proud. So am I - he looks so happy.

Like an infatuated groupie, Dreyfus hangs on my every word, eyes shining with admiration for the quality of my utterances, following me from room to room so as not to miss any profound statements that may escape my lips. I feel like his guru. When I speak, I hear his tail thump on the floor by my feet -" Right on, mudder!"

We have even developed a nightly routine. When I go to bed, dogs at my heels, Dreyfus immediately re-invades my personal space while standing at the side of the bed, head resting on my shoulder, tail wagging, trying to catch my eye, and stays a full ten minutes while I, helplessly, indulge him with a head and neck massage. I am unable to read through my fogged glasses, so endure the boredom as long as possible, before saying" Okay, now. You go to bed, Dreyf." And, I swear this is true: Dreyfus gives my cheek a tiny, gentle lick and retires with a thump and a sigh to his favourite bed. He's such an amazingly great guy - a people dog, a socializer - who spent so much time alone. But - he's okay now!

SO I HERD!

When a friend and I were talking the other day about why my dogs are sometimes so unsettled and restless when they should be resting in the house, I sensed he had a culprit in mind: Hogan! We've always believed that "A good dog is a tired dog." and take great pains to see that our dogs and foster dogs get plenty of exercise. This, I think, is the most common reason for dogs, especially large-breed dogs, developing behaviour problems. When I see clients whose dogs are giving them difficulties, my first question is "How much exercise does he get every day?" The most common response is "I don't walk him - he just lays around and does what he wants." Hmmm!

A large-breed dog, bred for hard work, lying around with no outlet for his vast stores of energy - becoming bored, restless, frustrated, irritable! Looks like a recipe for misbehaving. Those large dogs were meant to work - to hunt, to pull, to retrieve, to herd, to chase, to guard and (my favourite) to carry casks of brandy to people in the Alps. All those jobs require large energy expenditures. That energy being stored in your couch potato needs an outlet, whether it is a long walk or a rousing game of fetch. The energy needs to go there, rather than into destructive or aggressive responses.

During our discussion about trying to settle our dogs when they are in the house, a problem that we have had lately, the friend looked accusingly at Hogan, the Border Collie, and said "You don't see Border Collies in Cesar Milan's pack!" (The Dog Whisperer, National Geographic TV), implying that Hogan is the only reason that our pack is not as well behaved as the Dog Whisperer's. "*Ah-ha!*" I thought. "*Hogan's extreme activity, although normal for his breed, is getting to him!*" Just then, Hogan lifted his head and glared straight at my friend, as if to say "I herd everything!" He's so smart and so active that he can be annoying. I love his mind.

My grandfather used to say that his Border Collies were smarter than a couple of my brothers. So is Hogan. (I won't name names, but if you know them, I'm sure you can figure it out!) Yes, he's one smart puppy, but has a compulsive desire to work. For him, it is punishment not to be allowed to work. Short of becoming a sheep rancher, the best I can do for him is to try to keep his mind and body active. So, we're learning to dance and we play ball so much that I no longer "throw like a girl." We also join the other dogs in their daily walk, and then he plays with any dog who has enough energy left to play with him. That makes him tired (and cuddly) during the evenings.

On days when his ball game is called due to weather, Hogan becomes restless, compulsive, heedless, and, frankly, can be quite irritating. He paces, prodding the other dogs, annoying them (and us). He seems to change from the sweet, eager little guy that I know and love into someone else. He's sort of like a sullen, disappointed teenager. He's remote, self-centred, and when spoken to about his disruptive behaviour, instead of saying "Whatever!" as many teens do, his expression seems to say defiantly, "So I herd!" He'll be going for a really long run tomorrow.

WHO, IF NOT YOU?

The cat-making machine has been turned on again this year. It's late winter and tomcat thoughts are turning to queens - and the queens are ready. That is, the ones who have not been spayed or neutered. Fuelled by hormones, the wheels of conception and gestation are turning and soon batch after unwanted batch of helpless kittens will be moved down the assembly line that produces suffering and despair. Thanks to those whose intact cats are allowed to breed, the conveyor belt is never-ending. So is the suffering.

One unspayed female allowed on the streets can have up to three litters per year, with four or five kittens per litter. Those kittens born early this spring can be producing litters by early fall, at five or six months of age, and have years of potential for producing hundreds of kittens. In no time, your breeding cat and her "grandkits" can overwhelm a community, a shelter or a rescue. The time to spay is when you have one unspayed cat. You *know* that she is going to start having kittens, and you know that there are not enough homes for the cats already here.

Please don't abandon your unspayed cat where the *lucky* owner of a barn inherits your responsibility, discovering that he has an extra cat when she comes with kittens, starving and begging for food. (Yes, we know that happens, having rescued and spayed/ neutered many friendly, trusting, cuddly, confused and emaciated cats from cold barns.)

Here's a news flash: unless the barns are filled with cattle or horses, and insulated, you are not leaving the cat in a "nice, warm barn." You are leaving it to freeze in a nice, freezing, frigidly cold, unheated building.

Second news flash: the cat will not be fine, surviving on "all the mice" in that freezing barn. Does your house cat even know how to hunt effectively? The cat will struggle, frightened and confused, painfully cold, and slowly starving. Ears, toes and tail tips will freeze and fall off. Yes, it *is* true - I see it every winter!

Many barn owners whose own cats are spayed and neutered must now devote their resources to looking after your cast-off animals. Why, you ask? Because those good people cannot stand by and watch the consequences of the cruel abandonment. They will not allow that kind of suffering to occur. They have a heart!

But then, should your abandoned cat survive the winter until now - breeding season - she then gets to try to feed not only herself but the kittens that she carries. How can your tossed-away house cat do that? The truth: without help from a kind barn owner, she can't. She and her kittens become food for predators, die of starvation, or due to her poor body condition, she dies during labour, or the kittens die because she is unable to produce milk for them. She can't win. Here are the most humane answers to her plight:

1. Always, *always* spay or neuter your cat before six months of age;

2. Never, *ever* abandon animals on the streets or "in nice warm barns with lots of mice;"

3. If you find animals struggling to survive in our winters, feed them. Try to bring them inside. If not you, then who? They need help! Find homes for them. Raise funds to have them "fixed." Borrow our live traps to catch them before they become cat-making machines who perpetuate this cycle; and

4. If you can't bring them inside, build insulated shelters for them. Go to www.alleycat.org for information on helping stray or feral cats.

If you don't, then who will?

A DUNROAMIN' SITUATION

Please believe me when I say that there is no need for your pets to be reproducing. There are so many unwanted pet animals around this community that it is criminal to bring more into this world. Check out the local shelters, DunRoamin', or even, this week, my house.

With very little forethought, even less logic and planning, and in a frenzy of altruistic fervour, we seem to have gotten ourselves into what we call *a situation*.

Recently, when it became very apparent that Jerry, the Shepherd, was undeniably an itchy, allergic dog requiring special diet and daily medications, we decided that his chances of being adopted were so low as to be negligible. So, we like Jerry and we adopted him. Admirable, you may be thinking. Well, he makes seven miscreants and misfits who are officially *ours*.

That was last week, before DunRoamin' got another poor little thin cold dog with frozen ears and tail. She needed a place to stay where she would be warm and well-treated- fed, even. Then, we heard about an old dog, recently rescued, who had never been treated well and was blind. Now, this one is all my friend's fault! He has a soft spot for old dogs and as he says, "We're already looking after one old guy, our Mick. Might as well bring him here for the short time he has left, instead of living in a shelter." He needs to know life can be good. I agree, but the timing could be better!

Then came the DunRoamin' puppies. Six little seven-week-old unwanted pups. (It's not the owner's fault - dogs come and breed their female while she is tied in their own yard!) Luckily for us, two of our friends each offered to foster two pups. We instantly agreed before their brief flashes of insanity passed, and we gave them the dubious honour of being puppy foster parents.

So, how are we doing, you might wonder? Well, things are active with twelve dogs. I'm house training two eight-week old puppies, a one-year old pup, and a fourteen-year old blind dog. I'm no longer allowed to move any furniture since it upsets Ike, the blind dog. Not that I think it matters, since along with the non-moving furniture, he still has to contend with all the other constantly-moving canine objects. But, they are all adapting. Instead of jumping to their feet in angry disbelief that Ike has actually stepped on them, the dogs just growl, "Go around!"

And I've recovered what appears to be all the batting that was once inside the old comforter that I placed as a bed for the two pups. It's hard to tell for sure, when it is mixed with torn bits of wet newspapers, body excretions and shredded towels. I hope they didn't eat any of it, but I'm sure it will all come out in the end.

Brooklyn - of the frozen ears and tail - is doing very well with the house training and is very happy to be indoors and warm. She is so happy, in fact, that her tail never stops wagging and she's so enthusiastic that she constantly wags it against solid objects. Endearingly cute, but a sharp rap of her tail against my grandmother's old trunk split the end of her swollen, frost-bitten tail and started it bleeding. Still enthused, she continued her wagging and rapping which caused cast-off blood spray to dot the entire wall of the den opposite my chair and continued down the hall and into my bedroom. I don't think that the four tail bandages that she has eaten will bother her digestion, but I am relieved to have found a bandage that she considers inedible.

Then the darn pup pulled on one of Brooklyn's ears with a similar result from that swollen, weeping tissue. I've gotten the head shaking under control, though, and I think the bleeding has stopped for now. I didn't realize the force of her headshakes could cause blood spatter clear to the ceiling! After spending some time convincing our house cleaner, that our living quarters were not a crime scene, that we had not participated in a gruesome murder and that all the blood spatter evidence could be easily explained, she has agreed not to call in the authorities. She will not go to our basement, though.

And the pups - they have gone from cold, wormy, hungry, frightened little waifs to demanding little tyrants. Feed us!

Let us out! Pick us up! We want to play! Thank goodness for Hogan. Now he has something to herd, and more power to him.

IKE

It seems that some people are wondering why someone would take on a very old, blind dog, one whose entire life has been hard, and whose owners have given him very little care. Well, why not? It's not that difficult. You just need to take a little time - time to walk slowly (so the old dog can keep his neck in contact with your leg, so you can be his seeing eye dog), time to warn him of changes in elevation of the land ("Careful!" works for us) or time to guide him around obstacles or freshly-dug holes. You need a little time to earn his trust, a little more to teach him your routines, and some more to show him that he is always safe with you. After that, it's easy. After all, he's old, he sleeps a lot.

Now, after the first few weeks, I have time to observe the change in his demeanor - to notice how his head is now held high instead of fearfully low, how his steps are now careful, not tentative, and how his tail wags that entire end of him instead of just a small, meek movement of the very tip. I notice the change in his facial expression. Yes, his eyes are still unseeing, but he now smiles and his tongue lolls to the side of his relaxed jaw. He rolls on his back for a tummy rub and makes dog angels in the snow when we go out for walks. He now loudly berates the puppies when they tag team him and pull at his tail. He actually trots towards us when we come home, guided by the slapping noise that we make by hitting our legs with an opened hand. He tells us when he wishes to go out and where he wants to sleep. Yes, we put extra safety rails on the deck - low ones, and sides on the ramp leading up to the deck, to prevent accidents and it did take a week or so to house train him, but he's blind, not stupid. He has the idea now and we haven't had a problem in a couple of weeks.

Ike is amazing! After years of neglect and abuse, he is amazing. He still trusts. He is still interested in having a relationship with people. He still has a sense of humour. He can still play. No one can change the past, but it is the future that counts for Ike and for all the strays and rescues. The small amount of time and effort that it takes to reach out to a companion animal in need, or a person, even, is always worth it. By neglecting and denying Ike's need for a loving guardian, that previous guardian missed this great dog's smiling face, his wagging tail and his goofy grin. He missed having Ike lean on his leg, and lay his head in his lap. And he missed Ike's snow angels.

ITCHY

In March of 2012 we had a sad day at DunRoamin' Stray and Rescue. We lost one of our favourites, suddenly and without warning. We lost a good friend who had been with us for four years, and who never lost his charm and his appeal. We lost Itchy!

You see, he wasn't just a pretty face or a cute little cuddle bug. He was a good friend, a perfect gentleman. He had class. He had style. His wardrobe alone was impressive, but on his little back, a simple golf shirt was outstanding.

We first met him a few years ago, when he was brought to be euthanized, his skin disorder so severe and so itchy that he had scratched until his entire body was raw and bleeding. Looking beyond the traumatized, raw skin, his doctor saw something else - a kind, gentle, loving spirit, an old soul. At her request, he was relinquished to DunRoamin', and DunRoamin' was smitten.

After a few failed attempts to control his discomfort, Itchy was driven to the Atlantic Veterinary College in PEI to see a dermatology specialist, because . . . well, because he was Itchy! He was not just uncomfortable; he was our main man, Itchy.

Specialist recommendations eased some of his discomfort, but he was never able to discard the tiny shirts that prevented him from scratching his shoulders raw. Despite the uncomfortable skin, Itchy was always in a good mood. He took time to play with the stray kittens at DunRoamin' and showed them what "cool" really meant.

The clinic staff pampered him, loved him and looked after him well, despite his one unpleasant habit of producing many obnoxious odours. It could be heard throughout the building: *"Ohhhhh, Itchy!"*

Lynn was his favourite and it was mutual. In early February, Lynn decided that it was time for Itchy to live a regular life in a home, with a family - hers! He was having some health problems, perhaps due to his medications, and we all wanted the little guy to have a normal life.

So, our celebrity, our favourite and the favourite of our clients, former ditch cat, moved in with his favourite person and became family. His life there was happy and he always had his favourite - Lynn. Although short, I think he had a good life, despite his medical difficulties. He was safe and warm, well fed and an important member of a family.

We'll all miss him and his visits to the clinic. I'll miss being told "Itchy's here!" and seeing that face. Whenever I think of Itchy, it is with his wide eyes looking out from that little orange face - and wearing his favourite bright red baseball shirt!

WHY DO WE DO THIS?

Today, as I look around, I think, *"It looks like a dog exploded in my livingroom!"* I'm talking about the dog hair. There is dog hair everywhere - one of those signs of spring, or fall or summer or Thursdays, whatever. Sometimes as I walk around the house, dog hair swirling round my ankles, I wonder "Why do we do this?"

Today, I've taken the question seriously. And the answer? Schroeder. He's a black and tan pup, the result of an owner's refusal to spay her dogs, one of several litters in the past year. He arrived, after a long drive in sub-zero weather, with his freezing, terrified littermates, in an open wire crate on the open back of a big, shiny, new truck. They can't afford to spay his mother. It's not their fault. It's not Schroeder's fault either, or the fault of his littermates but, they, along with their mother, will pay the price. The pups are "Okay now." Three of the litter have been adopted into great homes. The other three are in foster homes awaiting the day when they will get their own family.

Like his littermates, Schroeder has now realized that there is more to humans than he originally thought. He now finds that he likes being with them and going on exciting adventures, such as the one he took to the farm the other day. He was particularly struck by the size of the horse. If it had moved, I don't want to think what Schroeder would have done. All that house training, gone to waste!

We smiled proudly yesterday when Shroe came in from outside, calmly walked over to our visitor, Pete, and without hesitation or invitation, climbed into his lap for a guy's bonding session. Not one to gush over anything, Pete was totally disarmed. As he met Schroeder's calm, level, inquisitive gaze, Pete exclaimed, "This is a nice pup!"

Pete's right. At eleven to twelve weeks, it is clear that Schroeder will be a big dog. He's at that stage now where the bones in his legs are huge, while his body hasn't quite caught up. He looks like one of those little trucks that people equip with huge, wide tires. But more than that, he's so calm, so observant, so intelligent. He has impressed us, as has the entire litter. I don't mean to imply that he's Superdog (but I do think he's super), just that he is all goodness - trusting, intelligent, calm, happy to be my companion, eager to learn the ways of the world. He has so much potential. He could be the best dog ever. Nature has given us this great pup! Now, our part, nurture, will determine if he reaches his potential. Schroeder and his littermates now need the guidance of their guardians in their permanent homes to learn how to live in today's world as happy, safe and content pets. They need training to understand acceptable behaviour. They need security, love and companionship - just like we do. They need to be cherished family members. They need to escape the loneliness that exists on a chain.

So, why do we and thousands of others do it? So Schroeder and millions like him can find the homes they deserve, homes that deserve them! So Schroeder is not wasted, suffering and languishing - on a chain!

ROYALTY

Before you ask- no, I did not get up early to watch the royal wedding the other morning. I hardly care what I wear, let alone what some princess on the other side of the ocean wears! No surprise, but my interest in Princesses extends to those who spend their lives tethered outside, unspayed and unwilling consort to any roaming Prince who happens by, nursing puppies who will never know the splendour of living in their warm castle with their own loving family. I am also interested in the Dukes who live, chained and alone in the backyard, ignored by neglectful owners. Where's the nobility in that? I worry about the Duchesses, abandoned and struggling to survive in cold barns, doomed to start their own "Barn" dynasty of short-lived struggling kittens as they reign over their poverty-stricken kingdom. The people who abandon them there should be crowned! What about the Ladys? Even with their high-born pedigrees, they are not impervious to neglect and abandonment. Royal blood is not, in and of itself, a guarantee of safety in life.

In a world of my choosing, each pet would be treated in a respectful, benevolent manner by august guardians to whom their well-being is paramount. I would love to see these grand and noble creatures (dogs) all living with honourable and humane gentlemen and women who are appreciative of the majestic splendour of the dogs' character and honour, and who laugh at his willingness to be the court jester.

Cats, too, of course! Although they themselves can display imperious and imperial attitudes, peering down their patrician noses at the lesser mortals who are often their guardians, and attempting to lord it over the world, they, too, deserve benevolent treatment. Even amid their loud disapproval that the throne is not up to their exacting standards, these litter queens - I mean 'little' queens, must be treated with deference. Although it is well known that rescued cats can change from "pathetic ditch cat" to "Queen of the World" with two weeks of supportive treatment, it is not for us to question the majesty of this transformation.

Our mission, as unquestioned lord and master to our dog friends, lowly servile commoners to prosperous, well-healed felines and short-term, temporary noble saviours to recently-rescued cats, is to ensure that they live fine, acceptable, meaningful lives under our guardianship. At risk of being a royal pain, let me reiterate yet again, that we do that by providing proper care for these animals that exist in our domains and that we prevent the suffering of unwanted pets

Until Each One Has a Home

by having our own pets spayed and neutered to help curb the pet overpopulation!

DYING FOR ATTENTION

I see them out there. It is one of the most terrible things that can be done to a dog - chaining him outside.

Forcing a dog to live away from his human goes against every instinct that your dog has, hence all the barking, whining, crying, pacing and clawing that dogs do when tied outside alone. That is not who a dog is, and it is not what a dog is for. A dog is a companion animal. The companionship is as important, if not more important, to the dog than it is to you. You have others for companionship as well. Your dog has only you, and not even you if you chain him outside.

Outside, he is a prisoner. Nothing more. He can't even move to increase his comfort, or find shade or water. His doghouse becomes an oven in summer. That's why so many dogs dig under their houses - to be in the cool earth and to escape the hoards of black flies, deer flies and mosquitoes.

A lone dog, tied in your back yard, alone and lonely, hurt and bewildered, sad and missing the one thing he needs most in this world - his person, lives in Hell. What kind of person maintains that suffering?

If you have a pet, you are responsible to ensure that that animal is:

1. Free from hunger and thirst.

2. Free from discomfort (physical and emotional)

3. Free from pain, injury and disease.

4. Free from fear and distress, and

5. Free to express normal behaviours.

That's why your dog needs to live inside. There should be no dog who lives outside unless you, too, live outside. And, I have to say that most people would not live in the conditions that outside dogs do.

Because dogs were chained in the past, doesn't make it right, then or now. Please, if you are going to chain dog outside, don't get one! If you won't bring him inside, be kind enough to give him to someone who will.

Saint Francis of Assisi said *"If you have men who will exclude any of God's creatures from the shelter of compassion and pity, you have men who will deal likewise with their fellow men!"*

GULLIVER

I finally caught him. I felt so bad that I was the cause of his distress. He was so scared in that trap. I've been feeding him for six months or so and worrying about where he went for warmth over this past winter. At least I know that he had food.

I call him Gulliver because, you know, he travels. When he's hungry, he lets himself be seen on the south-facing veranda of the old abandoned house near my home. I thought that he was just soaking up the warm sun on cold winter days but he still does it, even though winter is long gone. I now consider it his signal to me: "I'm back and I'm hungry." When I see him, I turn and drive back home to prepare his meal – a large bowl of dry food and a full can of wet food. He sees me coming, knows my voice as I call, "Kitty, Kitty," but cannot summon up the nerve to wait on the veranda. He slinks beneath it but stays nearby.

I deliver his food and, like a well-trained serving person, immediately make my exit. I glance back and note that he is eating before I even reach my car. "Eating" is a rather refined word for Gulliver's behaviour, I think. More accurately, he is using his lower jaw as a shovel, scooping large quantities of wet food into his mouth and swallowing mightily. At this point he is not even chewing. That's why I buy him the slivered chicken and fish – so he won't choke. Having observed this before, I know that soon he'll slow down and actually taste the food. By the time he starts on his dry portion, he'll be eating slowly, crunching the hard food and actually enjoying the flavour. Still, his head continuously turns from side to side, eyes alert for danger.

The last time I saw that, including the scars from fighting and the torn ear, Gulliver's eyes are very inflamed and I note large amounts of discharge. I thought that he was limping, too. He's wily and has little use for people except as food servers every three or four days. Where is he on other days? Doing what un-neutered semi-feral tom cats do, I suppose, fighting over girls, trying to get lucky, trying to keep ahead of predators, avoiding humans, cars and dogs, trying to keep warm, trying to stay alive.

With his obvious health issues, I'll try again to trap him the next time he shows. I'll put tempting food in the live trap and hope that he's hungry enough to make the mistake that will allow me to catch him for treatment.

So, I got him. He's neutered, vaccinated for rabies and the cat viruses, given long-acting antibiotics for his infections, treated for his horrific worm burden, ears cleaned, broken tooth removed and abscess cleaned.

I've set him up in one of my buildings until he's healed enough to go back outside. He will not allow me to see him now, hiding in the building and only coming out to eat when no one is around. He's close to his old hunting grounds so eventually I'll leave the door opened. My hope is that he will use the building as a home base. I've placed warm beds, catnip and lots of food in an easily-accessible spot. I don't want him to be a frightened prisoner. I only want to help if he'll let me.

I want him to have a warm place to sleep this winter, safety from predators and lots of food. He will likely do better now that he will no longer be obsessed with girls. Even as an outdoor feral cat, he can still enjoy some of life's luxuries. If he'll let me, I can easily provide them.

THEY SURE CAN MULTIPLY

Last year there was one stray female cat there. DunRoamin' was full, the cat was healthy, so was not taken in. We look after injured, sick, abandoned, neglected, abused or neonatal stray cats. We did offer to pay half the cost to spay her, though, but the offer was abruptly declined. Who spends money on cats? So, that cat had two daughters. Yesterday, DunRoamin' received all three cats and their three litters of tiny kittens, a total of fourteen cats. This was done to save their lives. The person who brought them would have spent more money feeding these cats over the winter than what it would have cost to have the original cat spayed - at full price! But, a quick drop-off and they are someone else's problem.

Let's see. Last year we would have been on the hook for one, or even three spays, up to three sets of vaccines and one-month boosters, three rabies vaccines, three flea and ear mite treatments and three dewormings - max. Then, they'd be healthy cats in a stable, non-reproductive population, needing only food and monitoring for illnesses.

Now, from that one cat, DunRoamin' (not the owner) is on the hook for - let's see: eight spays, six neuters, fourteen sets of vaccines, fourteen one-month boosters, fourteen rabies vaccines, twenty-eight dewormings, flea and earmite treatments, plus food and lodgings for fourteen extra cats, as well as recruitment of volunteers not only to care for these cute little guys, but also to start additional fund-raisers to meet the costs of spaying and neutering and feeding them all. That results in twenty-eight times the original cost estimate made last year. If that original cat had been spayed (at half the regular price), look at the difference it would have made!

Yes, they are very cute, mothers and babies alike. Yes, they are here and we have to help them, but these litters could have been so easily prevented! With already about seventy-five unwanted cats cared for by DunRoamin' (that's without counting the pregnant stray who delivered six kittens within minutes of her arrival last Thursday) we fundraise constantly to support them.

Those fourteen are over and above the actual, real, stray, desperately-struggling cats out there who have no guardians, the ones that DunRoamin' was set up to help.

Until society learns to prevent pet overpopulation, it is a societal problem. That means we are all on the hook for the suffering of our excess pets. That means that we all are responsible for these situations, these strays.

Yes, you need to feed that one struggling stray cat, you need to have compassion. Then you need to have the common sense to realize that cats multiply and take the proper steps to prevent more litters, most especially if you have assistance offered to help you do that!

DunRoamin' would have helped with this spay. Cost to us then: more hours of fund-raising to pay for that one spay. Cost to us now: many, many hours of fund-raising, many weekends given up to do spays and neuters, hours and hours of networking to find good homes for these guys and many sleepless nights, wondering how we will pay for the care that these fourteen, plus our real strays need, and worrying about what will happen to them if homes cannot be found. Or - what if an injured stray comes into our already packed non-shelter? We do not have a building. We rely on foster homes.

With all these unwanted and needlessly breeding cats, will we be able to help the strays that it is our mandate to help?

BRINGING HOME THE STANLEY PUP

I don't think that I've ever seen such a totally terrified dog. I've seen many frightened and panicky dogs, but none like this one.

He was so frightened that he couldn't run away. His eyes were huge, as big as saucers, as they used to say. His pupils were completely dilated by the extent of his fear. He had a deep furrowed wrinkle between his eyes marring his otherwise smooth brow, a sign of extreme canine stress. He couldn't even move when his would-be rescuer approached him, responding at the last moment with a small lunge forward and a short, unimpressive growl. He was almost catatonic!

He didn't respond to my attempt at a calm, soothing voice - my *dog* voice, either. The next step was to use my version of canine body language to try to calm his fear. Dogs use body language to communicate. The way they move, eye contact, head position and stance all have important meaning to dogs.

Employing my version of all the dog calming signals and behaviours that I knew, I approached the pup with my body sideways to him, using a c-shaped path and without making eye contact. I then squatted to make myself less threatening, slowing my approach even more. A quick glance in his direction showed that he was still very frightened, but his brow was less furrowed. I chose to take that as a positive sign, given that the mosquitoes had already taken multiple chunks from my exposed skin and the one in my peripheral vision chewing on my cheek looked like a monster. They were also feasting on the pup, and had been for some, I suspected. I remembered that dogs try to elicit calm from others by yawning – a signal of benevolent intent. I began to yawn widely, opening my jaw as I have seen Hogan do when I get angry, telling me, "Calm down, mudder!" I continued to try to calm him, barely restraining myself from covering my mouth with each jaw-cracking yawn.

He sat still and just stared. Still squatted in front of him, trunk carefully tilted away from him – in doggy invitation to come closer, still careful not to make prolonged eye contact, I slowly lowered the loop of the leash over his head and gently tightened it around his neck. He sat like a rock. I gave a gentle tug. He moved slowly toward me. Taking advantage of his momentum, I steered him toward the open door of the car. He leapt inside as I breathed a sigh of relief. By the time we arrived home, we were on the way to becoming best friends!

A physical exam told me a little about him – less than a year, intact male, slightly overweight, long pointed nails, sloppy, loose movement, little muscling in his thighs and legs, wavy, brindle coat, black muzzle and chest. This little guy was left on the Dump Road, a remote, wooded area that passes through the mountains behind Florenceville and meets the Bristol part of the community. He was noticed shortly after being dropped there, luckily for him.

He was so happy to have company and to play with the other dogs here that in no time he was exhausted. Still, he couldn't seem to settle. He seemed so happy to be with someone, to not be alone. He was over-stimulated, very excited, and determined not to be left alone. He stayed that way for three days, sleeping only when there were people or dogs with him, instantly alert for any movement in the area. He seemed happy, but unable to process all the activity around him. I sympathized, having felt the same at times with the twelve dogs here.

I have come to my own conclusions regarding this pup's previous life. I speculate, with some evidence, that this little guy has spent most of his young life confined and alone. He's very familiar with crates and dog runs. He's been well fed physically but has been craving companionship, attention and exercise. His eager attempts to solicit attention by jumping up no doubt contributed to his isolation. After six days of *normal* living, with plenty of exercise and socialization and learning our routines, he's not hard to handle at all. He is very aware that if you jump on people, they turn their backs or walk away, but if you sit politely, that unfailingly results in hugs and lots of petting. He knows that you can be rowdy outside but must confine yourself to less strenuous pursuits while indoors. He knows that strangers are a great source of cuddles and pets, if you remember to sit first. He knows that he's okay now.

I know that he's okay now as well. Still, I can't help but flash back to the night of the Stanley cup playoffs, when the Stanley pup was first found, that absolutely terrified little face, with no idea how to cope in the strange frightening forest, no survival skills at all, not even knowing if he could trust the strangers who were trying to help. I also know that packs of coyotes roam those woods and that they would relish a nice, fresh kill!

But, I also know that it was not the time for Stan to go. He needs to get a good home and live the long life to which he is entitled, with a good human friend worthy of a dog of Stanley's calibre. Then, and only then, will little Stanley be ready to go.

PET OVERPOPULATION

Anyone interested in adopting one of our many kittens and cats this month? It is officially "Adopt A Cat" month and June was chosen because it is the month when all the unwanted kittens are left at shelters, dropped outside someone's home, abandoned in the woods, or found in bags in ditches or along river shores.

Yes, I know everyone has heard it all before. I have written about it many times, preached it, actually, to try to get people to understand the severity of pet animal overpopulation and to urge people to spay and neuter their animals, so that they, too are not contributing to the problem of unwanted pets.

The other day, I found something written by the American SPCA and published by the Los Angeles SPCA which shocked even me. We see this problem at work on a daily basis - unwanted and abandoned animals. We *know* that it is a huge problem, but this article took my breath away.

It stated that, in order for all the animals now in shelter situations in the United States to find homes, every single American person would have to adopt fifteen dogs and forty-five cats. That means that in the States, a family of four would have to own two hundred and forty animals (dogs and cats) to give homes to those companion animals that are presently homeless. Mind boggling!

I don't have figures on homeless animals in Canada, but don't see much reason to think that we are doing much better than the American people. Even if the numbers are only half those quoted in the article, or even a third, the numbers of animals, per capita, are outrageous. We are both pet-loving nations. Our societies are similar.

So -here comes kitten season. If your pet is having kittens, please think about the effect that is having on the overpopulation problem. The only way to stop this is to line up for your fifteen dogs and forty-five cats – or stop the production.

OVERSTOCK SALE!

June is the month of savings at DunRoamin'. Due to an influx of product, we are extending our sale and having the biggest clearout ever! These are the lowest prices of the year! We're looking for owners for many tiny, abandoned but purrfectly beautiful little items. Don't miss this event – they are going at two for the price of one! They are all perfect! Double your value, double your fun!

We also have some of last year's stock available – the classics, those that never go out of style. Come and check out the elegant forms, the luxurious fur and the pleasing presentation. These ones are known for their exquisite performance and unmatched style with exceptional characteristics that ensure easy care and long life. Most have no-sag apparatus, for long-term durability.

We have just the perfect complement to the man's den or the man-cave. Come and see our rough, tough street toms

- the perfect accent to the games room, happy to lie on the couch and watch sports with you all day long.

As well, we have scratched and dented, and one-of-a-kinds, all available to just the right person. Mismatched groupings are now popular and we are sure that we have what you need. We have some of everything, so you can choose your own style!

Believe in the tried and true old-style family? We have entire families to fill up your house and make it a home where you are welcomed back each time you return, where you are the breadwinner, appreciated for your hard work. They'll sit in your lap and make you feel important. You don't even need to train the little ones – we'll send Mom along to do that for you!

Discover the luxury of our comfortable old over-stuffed cats. Get that homey feel immediately!

Don't miss the chance to add modern visual contrast to your home by adding stripes and splotches in many different color tones. We can match any decor and add richness and shine to your home.

Don't miss this once a year event!! We only have forty-five little ones, then they are all gone. The big ones are down to seventy and will be going fast in our great sale. Don't be left out! Drop in now while the selection is best!

PRICELESS DOGS

I don't know where all the dog hair comes from! I sweep it up, vacuum it up, pick it up, remove it from my food, comb it out of the dogs and I even vacuum some of them. (They don't like me to use the beater bar, though.) Still, it's everywhere.

If this were a fair and just world, I would have a thick, luxuriant mane of hair and all these dogs would be balding - and it would serve them right!

Not only that, but despite my repeated assurances that there is no hidden escape hatch in our bathroom, the dogs cannot rest while I am in there. Rather than listen to their pitiful whining outside the door, I have just let them accompany me on my private little trips. At present, due to the size, weight and sheer numbers of my canine followers, I am unable to close the bathroom door, not that I would have any privacy anyway, but...Gee!

Still, I've always been a proponent of multi-tasking and it has provided many a training opportunity for the dogs. From my seat in that room, I have taught the last four puppies to sit on command and five of my own dogs have learned to shake hands or give high fives. In this way the increased numbers have worked in my favour. Where, previously, a bored, unmotivated student could simply stand and walk out, I find that now, with all of us tightly packed in the small room, short of jumping in the tub, there is no escape route visible, and I have a captive audience for my teaching.

Oh, and I have found the sneakers that have been missing for so long, as well as two Kong toys, a Nylabone, a ski glove and a copy of "Prevention" magazine – all neatly piled under the ramp that leads onto our deck. I find it a somewhat odd choice of hidey-hole, since we all know that Ike, the old blind dog, urinates off the deck every morning at precisely that spot. I won't be keeping any of my things retrieved from there. I guess time will tell about the bone and Kongs – the odds are good that they will be playing with them tomorrow. That knowledge will force me to intervene and I'll probably run their toys through the dishwasher before giving them back.

Complaints aside, I always feel perfectly safe in their presence – whether it's walking on some isolated trail, or home alone at night. One would be a fool to try to break into a house with eleven dogs in residence (not to mention the fact that anything that once was valuable has probably already been chewed, broken or stolen by the dogs themselves.) Actually, that's not true. Everything that is valuable in this house is lying, sprawled and sleeping in the middle of the living room floor, content just to be in the same room with me, to be part of my life, and to be someone's dog. Even the foster dogs – they're happy to be my dog for now, until that permanent person comes along, the one they have been waiting for their entire lives.

SPAY IT FORWARD

Sitting here looking at the forty-some kittens that have been rescued from roadsides, abandoned in fields, or on the clinic doorstep (thank you very much), I can't help but agree completely with the experts who all agree on one thing (amazingly) - the answer to the pet overpopulation problem is unquestionably to spay and neuter pets! That is the whole answer.

If we would all do that, the problem of pet overpopulation could be solved, pet suffering could be markedly reduced, and the deaths of millions of lovely animals just like yours who are euthanized in shelters every year, could be prevented.

Here's a thought. If you have adopted an animal that is already spayed or neutered, why not "Spay It Forward?" You could do this by making a donation to cover the costs of surgery for someone else's pet - someone who at present is unable to afford it.

Recipients could be asked to commit to helping another pet surgery when they get a bit of extra cash (or after they have done a fund raiser – a bake sale, a bottle drive, etc. to raise the funds.)

Do you have a neighbour whose cat has litter after litter? Do you know someone who really loves their cat but is unable, right now, to spay her? Is there a neighbourhood stray who really needs help?

Start talking! "I see your cat has another litter. I'd like to help you get her spayed." Call a local clinic to set it up and send your part of the payment to the clinic on behalf of that person. Then, if the recipient of your kindness helps someone at a later date and that person helps someone else . . . see how it could help? For every cat spayed, literally thousands of births are prevented over the lifetime of that one animal and all her potential offspring. Thousands!!

The effects of your kindness mathematically measured in kittens NOT produced:

> Cat: Average years of fertility - 7
> Average number of litters per year - 3
> Average number of kittens per litter - 5

The result is the production of more than one hundred kittens birthed to that one cat. BUT, starting at five months of age, her kittens will be reproducing as well, her daughters producing their litters even as their younger sisters are being born.

This situation was easily evidenced in our recent article where people refused to spay one cat last fall, resulting in three cats with litters of unwanted kittens this year - fourteen unwanted cats!

Cats are great! They can't read or write, but they sure can multiply! Spay it forward!

JUST THERE

I think it is the most obscene tactile experience that I have ever encountered! To hold a small being in the palm of your hand, feel his soft baby fur - and only bones immediately beneath that fur. The senses are repulsed; the mind somehow unable to accept what the eyes see and the hand feels.

Kittens are supposed to be cute and soft and warm and cuddly – and fed! They are not supposed to be cold, and starved and dehydrated, like little JT. He was aware but too weak to walk, starved but too weak to eat, cold but with no fatty stores to warm him. He was dying, right there on the side of the road where he was found.

At the clinic, his little dry body was warmed on hot water bottles and by the body heat of the vet tech who held him close. He was given warm fluids under his skin as he was so dehydrated. When he had finally reached a normal body temperature, he was offered food. It had been so long since he had eaten, that he didn't feel the urge to eat. His tech forced small amounts of warm food into his mouth every half hour- life-saving, urgently required food.

Although he looked somewhat better at the end of the day, he still showed no desire to eat on his own. His tech took him home and continued forcing him to eat. The next morning he was warm, hydrated, a bit more alert –but still refused to eat on his own. This happens to kittens like JT. Their hunger centres don't seem to tell them that they need to eat - or they have concluded that it is hopeless. His tech told him forcefully, "You will eat if I have to force you for weeks!" She'd done it before. She'd lost some, won many and she wasn't giving up.

But – the next morning - she didn't have to force him! JT met her at his kennel door, eyes bright, demeanour alert, attitude saying "I'm gonna LIVE!" and "Bring on breakfast!" He devoured his meal on his own, pausing now and then to head butt with his grinning tech. At the clinic he entertained his fans by giving himself a good bath, attempting to play and then preparing for the great life that he had decided to live. He was sure that it would be much better than his first five weeks!

KITTIES ARE SO NICE

Give me a bunch of dogs any day. People always say that cats are so much easier than dogs. Don't get me wrong, I love cats. But, I now have three sick male kittens rescued from a local trailer park, where their litter mates were getting run over. The clinic basement is full, so . . . they are in my garage along with a mother cat (not theirs!). She was said to be feral, and therefore was supposed to get spayed and released back to her regular haunt. Not being feral changes everything, and now I feel honour-bound to find her a home.

Now, momma cat (or Auntie Griselda, as we call her) seems to tolerate me all right, even deigns to sit in my lap and purr, if I manage to get her accommodations to her exacting standards and have served the proper brand of stinking canned food. That is quite a step up for a cat that couldn't choke food down fast enough when she first came here – but, I've come to expect less adoration from the cats compared to that which I have received from my very appreciative dog friends.

The situation is a little different for the three little boys. I call them the Trailer Park Boys – and, if I'm any judge of cat expressions and vocalizations, their language isn't much better than that of their TV counterparts. Despite having taken great care in setting up their accommodations to the exacting standards of my sister, the Cat Whisperer, having hand-fed their favorite stinking fish food to them, tossed a multitude of tasty cat treats at them (I mean "to" them), and gently cradled them in my arms while petting their little heads and rubbing their little chins, they still hate me!

By this point, and after this much attention, I would have captured the heart and soul of any dog rescued from these dire circumstances and earned the undying love and gratitude of that canine, with half the work that I have put into these kittens. Still, they hate me! At least their little eyes are clearing up and look much less painful. And they are no longer the bony little waifs that I dragged home, but I don't see us being best friends any time soon. What am I doing wrong? Do I appear too desperate for their friendship? Am I trying to get too close too soon? I never have this problem with dogs.

When I look at my little Trailer Park Boys, I can't help but think that if every hiss was bleeped and every growl muted, our interactions would be very similar to those on the TV episodes. "How are my little kitties?" "Bleep! Silence! Leave me the bleep, bleep alone, you old bleep!"

In keeping with the theme and in desperation, I am thinking of trying one final maneuver to gain their friendship. I think I'll get them all hopped up on catnip from our garden, then slip under their mental barriers while their guard is down and they are trippin' on their weed. It could work - people say weed blocks their inhibitions. Nothing to lose, really, but my dignity – if I had any.

Despite Bubbles's (of the real Trailer Park boys) contention that "Kitties are so nice!" I'm afraid that unless we have a huge breakthrough with the catnip therapy, "nice" will not be the descriptor in our relationship.

NOBLESS OBLIGE

He'd been tied outside since he was a puppy, pacing, walking in circles, wondering what the world was like, if his people were all there was to "people." He had concluded that if they were what "people" were, the world couldn't be much.

At a year and a half, he was a beautiful, if frustrated, dog who had never really had a chance to run at his full speed, to tire himself out, and to explore the things that his nose told him were out there. One day a strange person came and took him away to a strange place. She said "I've been trying to *get* you for ages." He didn't know what that meant, but he liked the way she talked to him and patted his head. The second stranger said something about him being "finally free." They said he'd get a new name, something 'noble', and that he would get a new home. He didn't remember having an old name.

He was put in something called a "run" where he was dry and protected from the pouring rain. There was no mud.

Instead, there was a soft, padded bed that felt so good to lie on, and he was given something called a "chewy." He felt positively decadent!

He wondered about the other dog who had been tied near him. He'd never been able to touch him or play with him. The first person said that it had been twelve years that the old dog had been tied there. That's eighty-four dog years - winter and summer! His people had repeatedly refused to give up the old guy.

He wondered what his future held. He'd decided that he would rather die than live as his old friend had. He began to make his plans. Then a man opened the run and led him out into the rain. He said "Come on, Noble! Not another day is going to pass without you having a good run." The man took him to a large fenced field and released him. He just stood there. He couldn't remember not being restricted by a chain or collar. The man waited - then gave him a little push. "Go on, Noble!" The dog started to trot, then to run. Then he burst into a mad, crazy, figure of eight run, zig-zagging past the man, running with all his might and finally flopping on the man's sodden feet. The man made a play-bow. The dog responded, running madly in circles, buzzing past the man. He had never had this much fun and freedom in his life. He was sure of it! He noticed that the man was showing all his teeth – but he didn't seem aggressive. He seemed . . . happy. He decided that there was a lot that he needed to learn about men. He'd start with this one – after he finished running. Finally, exhausted from the unaccustomed exercise, the dog collapsed on the man's feet and accepted a treat." *This must be happy,*" he thought. He walked willingly and happily at the man's side as he was returned to his dry bed. Ah, the luxury. The freedom to run, the praise, the treats, the gentle pats, the companionship, the "Good boy, Noble!" and the soft, dry bed.

He thought of his old friend, still imprisoned by his chains, and wondered if he had ever felt like this. He couldn't know of the many people who had tried to have his friend released from his chains, to have him brought into the house – to have him experience a life! He couldn't know that people would continue their efforts to help his old friend. He couldn't know that the laws of the country don't protect dogs from the treatment that he and his friend endured. He also couldn't know that many people were working to try to change the laws so that dogs like Noble could have a good life.

Noblesse oblige – the obligation of those of high rank to be honorable and generous.

STANDARDS

Recently I saw a rather sad cartoon in which a dog asks, "If a dog barks his head off in the woods and no one hears him, is he still a bad dog?" That started me thinking and I came up with a few questions of my own.

I wondered: if a dog repeatedly hides and moves to escape the pinching of a child and, finally, trapped by the child, he snaps – is he still a "bad" dog? Is it necessary then, to kill this dog, because they *will not have a dog that will bite!*

If a dog doesn't return to his guardian when called, despite being hit for not returning before, is he a "bad" dog? Or is he smart enough to anticipate another blow from the same person this time?

If a puppy teases and mauls the cats when he is small, is it his fault that he still does it when he is big? Or should someone have taught him better behaviour towards cats?

If a young large breed dog doesn't get trained in obedience, is it his fault that he doesn't obey? And if he doesn't get exercised, is it his fault that he is disruptive?

If a dog is trained by someone who has never trained a dog before, is it his fault that his behaviour is not perfect?

If a dog whose instincts tell him to herd, chases a car or someone on a bicycle, is he vicious and does he need to be killed? What should he do with all those instincts if they are not redirected into a long run or a game of fetch?

If a dog is taught by someone who only adopted him because he was small and sweet and cuddly, is it his fault that he turns into an over-bearing adult?

If a dog is home-schooled by an inept instructor who doesn't know the curriculum or understand the student, is that, too, the stupid dog's fault?

If we had a mandatory school system for dogs with well-trained instructors, well versed in dog psychology and dog behaviours who taught them the life skills and behaviours required to live comfortably in our society - would people try to kill as many for minor behaviour lapses?

All that I can think now, is, that it's a good thing people don't have to meet the standards that some people set for dogs. Guess our prisons wouldn't be as full, if we did—but our graveyards would.

DISENCHANTMENT RANT

I occasionally answer the DunRoamin' phone lines and have received many, many strange calls - some annoying, some heart-wrenching, some completely uninformed and some actually threatening - along with many legitimate requests for help for found animals who need veterinary care. I am happy to be a source of help for these animals who have not seen the best of mankind. DunRoamin' was created to assist injured, starved or sick animals who have no guardians to provide the needed care. This is our mandate.

I also have received many calls from well-intentioned people who are concerned for the healthy strays in their areas. They do not need more cats, but cannot allow them to starve on their very doorsteps, and yet are terrified about the next wave of kittens which everyone knows is due very soon. They would like us to take in these cats as well. We wish we could! We are all animal lovers or people who have no tolerance for the suffering inflicted on these products of irresponsible pet owners who will not spay and neuter their pets. We all want them safe, warm, fed, vaccinated, treated for parasites *and* we very much want them to be spayed and neutered. We want them in homes where they receive the care and the lives to which they are entitled. We worry about them all the time, as do our callers. We do what we can, but often it doesn't seem like enough.

The service that we provide for the stray, injured, sick and starving animals - community animals, *not owned animals,* costs us several thousand dollars every month. We must raise those funds on our own. We are not funded by the government nor assisted by any of the many municipalities from which we acquire our patients. We are nothing more than a group of individuals who will not accept the damage our society does by discarding little domestic pets to the harsh realities of the streets, the woods, old barns or back roads. We look after those that the existing (and overflowing) shelters are not medically equipped to care for.

We donate our services. These animals are taken to our homes to be monitored, to be fostered while they regain their health. Their doctors do their surgeries in their free time. Volunteers give up their mornings, their weekends, their sleep, their free time to allow this organization to function - all for society's cast-offs. We all know that it is wrong to place so little value on a life and to care so little about suffering. We must try to help and we know that we have made positive changes in the lives of these animals for whom we have claimed responsibility.

BUT- I digress.

Sometimes it is hard *not* to become disenchanted with some of our callers and visitors asking for help from DunRoamin'. This little rant was brought on by an accumulation of events over the past few weeks, and the final straw called about an hour ago. The message stated that the caller had taken in a stray kitten several months ago and she wanted DunRoamin' to *fix* it for her. If we couldn't *help* her, she said, she would not be interested in keeping the kitten. This just days after a stray was brought to us by someone saying that they didn't want a big bill, but if DunRoamin' (the non-profit, charitable organization staffed by volunteers) would take care of the cat's abscess and neuter and vaccinate the cat, they would adopt him.

It's hard to walk away from calls like this without feeling used! We constantly have to tell ourselves that *it is all about the animals*. I must never forget that. DunRoamin' will continue to help injured strays. Our volunteers will continue to donate their time to help us raise funds and take care of these strays. But we can't be expected to take care of every unowned pet out there. We need people to step up and take responsibility for their animals. And we need people to help us house, feed, and raise funds for the animals that they bring to us for help. You don't need medical staff to care for healthy strays, and if you adopt a healthy, stray cat, surely you can care for it properly and have it spayed or neutered without expecting a charity to do it for you.

PURRCEPTION

In attempting to come up with an interesting and new take on animal issues, I have found this week to be a catastrophe, as far as ideas go. I had intended to write something over the weekend, when someone noted, perchance, an emaciated grey cat in the vicinity of the clinic. Out came the live trap baited with lots of food and now "Purrchance" has settled his skinny, little, flea-ridden, burdock-matted butt into a soft bed in a warm kennel. Exhausted, he sleeps and eats alternately. He's so tired! "Sleep, Purrchance, to dream!"

Then my mind took a little side trip while I thought of all the ways we use cat adjectives and prefixes in our everyday lives. So many of our words start with "cat" or "pur."

Along that vein, I've decided that we could actually make good use of these words to subtly warn or inform our volunteers who regularly look after these guys, regarding some of the cat's personality issues. I think it could work. We really could start a "cat" language for the basement - just to add a little spice to life down there. It's easy! The volunteer who medicates the cats would be the "catterpiller." The catterwaul would be climbed by the felines to reach the window that opens into the cat run. A cat bed would be a "purrport" or a "purrch." A cat tug-o-war would be a "purrple." Within sight of the cats would be within "purrview." Cats running after each other would be a "purrchase."

And the cats themselves: a volunteer who needed to handle "Purrcuss" would be aware that he is likely to growl and vocalize in a hateful way. "Purrfume" would be a very angry, aloof cat. "Purrsnickity" would be very fastidious. When looking for "Purrson," one would know they were looking for a little male kitten. "Purroxide" would be a blonde-colored cat. "Purrmeate" would always be found by the food bowl, while "Purrjure" would be a liar! "Purrspire" would be a feline conspirator. And "Purrmafrost" would likely have lost her ear tips, having been found after a long period of sub-zero temperatures. Equally, "Purrlyte" would be very thin. Someone called "Purrpetrator" would be a bad fellow, and "Purrmit" would have huge paws with many extra toes. "Purrpetual" could never get enough petting and "Purrsuade" would have the softest, smoothest short coat! "Purrloin" would be a feline thief, and "Purrsue" would be a sissy male cat. "Purrgative" would be a little sh-t cat.

This is fun in a weird sort of way – but it's necessary that we realize that, if it was not for the purrsistant and catastrophic attitudes that purrmeate the area, it would not be necessary to intervene to save the lives of these guys and purrvent further suffering. Let's all purrsist in encouraging every purrson who is, purrhaps, lax in stopping the cat-making machine that is their cat, to please spay and neuter.

Okay! Let's call a spayed a spayed! That's the answer - purr and simple!

DUNROAMIN' TELEPHONE LOG, SEPTEMBER 2011

One was found under an abandoned
house, nursing several kittens;

One appeared outside a home;

One was abandoned in a closed apartment;

One, very pregnant, was found on
a remote dead-end road;

One was found on a woods road, with a broken leg;

One was thrown from a car and suffered major facial injuries;

One was found under a deck trying
to nurse her kittens;

Until Each One Has a Home

One was scratching at the window of a local residence;

One, half blind, followed someone for
a kilometer, hoping for help;

One was found on the front lawn of a local home;

Three were found in a ditch during a heavy rainstorm
– they had been seen there for the previous three days;

One was found in a closed basement,
no mother was ever found;

One appeared in a driveway;

One was found lying on the side of the road;

One was found unconscious in a parking lot;

One was crying at someone's door, asking for help;

One has been seen all summer outside an
apartment, and now looks very sick;

Two were left in an apartment when
the owners moved away;

Two were found on a lawn;

Four were found in a potato sack on the side of
the road, the mother with a dislocated hip;

Three are under an abandoned restaurant;

One was found on the doorstep;

One starving one was found outside the clinic;

Mildred A. Drost DVM

Six were found in a lumberyard;

Five more were found in the woods;

And one was found having kittens on an outside deck as the first snow of the season floated on the air.

iKAT BEATS AN APPLE EVERY TIME

Did you stand in line to get the newest Apple products as soon as they were released? The iPhone and all the newest highest tech stuff? What a waste!

There is already an ancient product that supplies all of those needs and more – and it is user friendly and compatible with any operating system.

Bet you don't believe me, do you? Well, at DunRoamin' we happen to have the newest forms of the ancient product that has more uses than anything Apple ever dreamed of!

For example –

> Need to get a smile on your face? There's a cat for that!
>
> Need someone to nap with? There's a cat for that!

Need soothing relaxing sounds to help you sleep? There's a cat for that!

Need to rid your home of rodents? There's a cat for that!

Need help perfecting your yoga stretches? There's a cat for that!

Need someone to play with? There's a cat for that!

Need an iPad lap stand? There's a cat for that!

Need a spiritual guru? There's a cat for that!

Need a morning wake-up call? There's a cat for that!

Need a hug? A lap warmer? There's one for that!

Need a paper shredder? There's a cat for that!

Need a cat scan? There's a cat for that!

Need a friend for man's best friend? There's even a cat for that!

Need a babe magnet? Yup, there's also a cat for that! (we call her Anne Shirley and is she ever cute!)

Need new Christmas ornaments? We have the cats for that!!

Need a new entertainment center? We have cats for that.

Need a wireless speaker, a portable scanner, an activity tracker, a sleep monitor, an active lens, or a quick clip –we have the perfect cats for that too.

Renowned for their versatility and ease of handling as well as their long life and battery function, this is one of the core reasons that they out-perform any Apple product in their class. The iKat.

Also, these models are locally grown and produced and are stored at the local warehouse –DunRoamin' Stray and Rescue.

Remember –buy local and watch out for a bad Apple.

ROGER

Have you heard about Roger? He's the old tomcat recently rescued and brought to DunRoamin' for care. His face is scratched and scarred. He has one cauliflower ear. His coat is dirty and brittle. His tail is stubby and bent. His body has scars from repeated fights and injuries. His muscles are stringy and tough. His body is lean and strong. He's a warrior who has fought for survival for his entire life. Until now.

Now he can let go of the constant vigilance that has been his entire life. He is no longer stressed by the weather or the demands of hunting for food. He knows where his next meal will come from. He luxuriates in the soft warm beds that are provided for him. He welcomes his friends daily and trusts that they have his well-being in mind. He gives back the love and attention that he receives.

Although he may not have the sleek elegance that is present in so many of the DunRoamin' cats awaiting adoption, he has many attributes that make him a great potential adoptee.

I have made a list.

1. He is user friendly and very interactive.

2. He is quite cheeky, in a tomcat sort of way.

3. He is one hundred percent nut free.

4. Adopting Roger saves two lives, his and the cat that he makes room for.

5. He's always up for a pawty.

6. He's no longer a fan of Sex and the Kitty.

7. He's a catalyst for good will.

8. He's an adult but not yet a senior kitizen.

9. He's a purfect gentleman.

10. Treated well, he's very unlikely to mewtiny.

11. He has experience in claw enforcement.

Think about it. As a roommate, he may even do light mousework!

WE'RE RESPONSIBLE!

Well, I guess we should talk about puppy mills and backyard breeders this week, in view of the recent SPCA seizure of all those poor little dogs, and in our own backyard, so to speak! This time we can't blame Ontario or Quebec or the states. This one is in New Brunswick – this one is on us!

These animals were not respected or protected in our own province. Shame on us! Oh, we're pretty good with our own individual animals, at least many of us are. But what about the dog who lived his entire life on a chain, the cats abandoned in the woods, what about these poor little mites? They all need protection and we have failed to provide it. Again. We have more stringent laws about whether people are allowed to see cigarettes in a store than we do to protect animal lives. These are living beings capable of suffering and for whom there are no choices. Is there a law that forbids us from seeing the conditions that these poor things must live in? If we can't see cigarettes, should we be allowed to see the squalor that was their home? We need to bring New Brunswick animal protection into the present and plan for the future. We need to bring changes to the way our government (and our population) view these living beings. We domesticated them, we want them, we are responsible for them - not just our own individual animals but animals in general.

Too many cats around? The answer is simple – don't allow them to breed! People won't spay and neuter? Legislate it! We have laws for much less important things. Dogs tied outside and starved? Prosecute it! Laws don't allow prosecution? Fix the laws! Make them better so that these abuses are stopped! I believe that is a big part of the answer.

But, you know, as much as it is nice to blame the government and disinterested legislators and inadequate laws, I don't think we can let ourselves off lightly, either.

Yes, that puppy in the pet store is cute. So is the pup sold in the Wal-Mart parking lot - but we all know where they come from. We know that good breeders don't sell pups like that. The DunRoamin' mantra applies again: "The dog (or cat) always pays!" Those parents of these little guys have paid – with matted coats, rotten teeth, caked feces, urine scalds and lifetimes of only confinement and reproduction. With this rescue right in our backyards, under our very noses, we should have smelled the trouble these animals were in. How could we have let this happen here – where we love our animals?

The truth is that to some people, dogs equal money, and someone paid money for all those pups without doing the necessary research. And what about Mom? I wish you could see her. The smell of just that one mother in my home permeates the entire house. The smell of old feces and urine; this, despite several thorough deodorizing baths. She still stinks! She's terrified, shivering, not house trained, afraid to eat, afraid to look at me, afraid not to look at me, totally unsocialized! She's exhausted, thin, raggedy. Her coat is dull and brittle. She's lame on one leg. Her bones protrude. She doesn't know if she can trust. She doesn't know what to do – or what I might do! She has no idea how to cope – or what the dangers are. She has no idea what she's seeing for the first time. She's been a prisoner, a production machine, a means to make more money, no matter what the cost to her. She doesn't know people, or trust, or good times. She doesn't know fun or walks or security. She doesn't know who to trust or even what trust is.

She does know one thing. She knows dogs, and now she knows Hogan. She knows she can trust the Border Collie, and she knows that for sure. He's her calm, secure, gentle, helpful big brother right now. She takes her cues from him. He's safe. She understands that. Maybe he can teach her to understand people and begin to trust.

What she went through so that they could sell pups! Why don't they just get a job?

IN THE DUNROAMIN' NEWS

The latest stray cat that we have taken in has a terrible story. She was abandoned, parasitized, terrorized, starved, shot (twice), hit by a car and, now, must have her horrifically damaged leg amputated. The only thing that I can say to that is, "Well, at least she wasn't stabbed, bludgeoned, shot from a canon, attacked by coyotes or shoved off a cliff (at least not that we know of)."

What we do know is that this young cat has lived through Hell, thanks to the people that she has encountered in her short little life. She is so traumatized that we are not yet sure whether she is terrified and shocked or if she is actually feral. If she is really feral and ends up with only three legs (we don't think we can save it due to the extreme damage), then what? Her odds of survival outdoors on three legs are almost nil.

A cat living outdoors must be always alert for danger, then very agile, amazingly quick and very speedy to survive. That cat must be a superb hunter, excellent at finding adequate shelter, constantly alert for dangers even when resting, and also have the luck of the Irish to make it through even one winter. That is a cat who starts the winter in good physical condition, well nourished, wily and aware of the dangers in his neighbourhood, a cat who has had time to learn survival skills. This little mite has three strikes against her before it even gets cold, and that is without factoring in the bullet wounds.

Now that she is in a rescue situation, her outlook has improved markedly. We hope that she can be a house cat. Even if she stays antisocial, it's the only way that she can live a safe, comfortable life. We have clients who have cats like her in their homes. One client sees her cat, on average, once weekly for a few seconds. She just enjoys the knowledge that this cat is safe, warm and fed, even if she is not social.

Do you have space to share with someone who only wants to live?

In other DunRoamin' news, the "Occupy Sofa" movement here at home instigated by puppy mill survivor, Taylor, continues. Although peaceful, local residents are becoming annoyed at the constant presence on the sofa and are pushing local officials to remove the protestor so that they can resume their naps in their usual comfort. Taylor has been "camping out" on the sofa for the last week to protest the huge disparity between the lives of puppy mill dogs relative to those of pet dogs. "Capitalism is the root cause of all the exploitation of our resources," she says, "including mine!" This small protester ably demonstrates that when we have had enough of the negative and destructive consequences of decision-makers, we have a responsibility to speak out. "I hope that my children, wherever they are, will join me in this protest!" she barked.

Taylor's Occupy Movement is taking its toll on the residents here, as she will not leave her sofa except when physically carried outside, and her passive resistance extends to refusing to walk on a leash. Residents are also appalled by the smell in the area, but steps have been taken to rectify that problem, with Taylor submitting to repetitive baths without complaint. "This is the stench of capitalism at its worst!" she cried as she emerged, sodden, from yet another shampooing.

"My sistas and I have been exploited for far too long! We need greater protection by the law and by those who choose to remain silent in the face of this treatment!"

Taylor is determined to camp out until her cause has been acknowledged and promises have been made to end this terrible oppression. Local residents, though, have become increasingly disturbed by the effect that this Occupy Movement is having on the sofa, citing fears of wear and tear on the fabric and resulting lumpiness from pressure not evenly distributed across the entire piece of furniture. Some say that the seams are starting to show strain as well.

CHRISTMAS POEM

After fostering numerous puppies recently, here's my version of "Please Come Home For Christmas:"

> My ears are still ringing, I need glad, glad news
> Oh, what a Christmas to have you puppies loose
> My mind is gone, I have no friends
> To help me clean up once again
> Oh, what I'd give for a silent night
> No puppies screaming by the fireplace light
> Please get a home for Christmas
> Please get a home for Christmas
> If not for Christmas, by New Year's night
>
> Friends and relations they show hesitations
> Even though my floors shine with bleach
> They say "This is Christmas
> Christmas is here, it's the messes that I fear
> What did I step in?" they screech!

Until Each One Has a Home

Please get a home for Christmas,
Please get a home for Christmas
If not by Christmas, by New Years night.

"Now will you tell me, since this is my home
Why you puppies are chewing on my memory foam? "
I don't want them to be frozen, starved or in pain
So I'd do it at Christmas, once again!
They won't have the sorrow, the grief or the pain
And I'll be happy—happy, even though I'm not sane
Please get a home for Christmas,
Please get a home for Christmas,
If not for Christmas, by New Year's night!

HEAT

Okay. So . . . no, I did not get the Christmas tree up and decorated this year. It seemed like an exercise in futility, what with two very hyper ten-week old pups who want to explore (i.e. chew) everything. Amazingly they are able to disappear in a virtual second and the adult, unmotivated dogs can't be bothered to find them. They are mostly to be found where they are forbidden to be – in the thirty-five-year-old yucca tree, in the laundry hamper, in the storage area for good dog treats (in case I get any good dogs) or in the garbage.

Also we're housing Belle, a nine-month old female dog in full heat. For those of you who are new to the language, that means that one second's inattention on my part while she has an intact admirer at hand and we will be the proud foster grand-parents of— oh, six, maybe eight grand-pups two months from now.)

I thought that this situation would be tolerable – all the other boys are neutered and old blind Ike is now almost fifteen and sleeps the better part of the day, only rousing for meals and bathroom breaks - BUT, since the arrival of the *in heat* dog, we have noted a surge in his daily activities. It appears that he is infused with a new zest for life upon realizing the opportunity that awaits him. I would have said that he didn't have it in him! And it's Christmas, not Easter!

I think perhaps, that I can be forgiven for underestimating the hormonal effect that would magically restore this old guy to his youthful vigour. I had anticipated some whining and maybe a little unfocused sniffing, but never this! I would also like to apologise to any neighbours who may have witnessed my pajama-clad body vaulting over the deck rails, heard my mind-chilling bellow of "NO!" and tracked my red attire on my beeline across the outdoor pen, hurdling to its farthest corner where Ike was positioning himself for success. By all appearances, he had a plan and only a smidgen of eyesight and a slip of my feet in the snow would have made it a done deal. The little hussy was upset to be hustled back into the house and returned to solitary confinement. "You can only chew so many bones!" she shouted as I firmly locked the door on leaving her room.

The soundproofing in the bedroom walls intended to dull the TV noise from the next room has certainly been useful over the holiday, the ear plugs as well. Benadryl (two for me and two for Ike) has helped me sleep and with "Adele" crooning in the background, you can hardly hear the persistent whining. *Who knew?* I guess *it* really is the last thing to go! Even the neutered dogs show a more-than-passing interest in the little female. They are very interested, but seem to forget why. I may go out of my mind. It's certainly been a whole different ball game here this week.

With all the commotion centered around the adult dogs, I've hardly noticed the puppy stuff – didn't need the lower leaves on that plant anyway, or those socks. Wiping up the floors is a pleasant break from rescuing Ike from his latest trap. I guess he forgot that he can't get all the way through behind the stove, and that you have to turn around to get out of the bathroom. His mind is elsewhere - and I'll be glad when it gets back!

I don't understand why anyone, why any dog owner would put themselves through these three weeks of hell. Did I mention the blood spotting all over the floors and the whining and howling of the neighbours' dogs, the lack of brain function in all the male dogs here, neutered or not? If you want puppies, rescue the many frozen, starved, neglected and abused ones in your area. Spare yourself the insanity of my last two weeks, spare yourself the costs of a caesarian section, and spare the world from the pain of excessive, unwanted pets. Your breeding pets add to the misery.

Oh, and speaking of misery – I will never willingly subject myself to this particular set of circumstances again! (Well, unless I have to.)

TEACH YOUR CHILDREN
(TWO- OR FOUR-LEGGED)

With all the puppies that DunRoamin' has adopted out over the years (and the many cats as well), we often have owners asking for advice on how to modify some behaviour problem or other. Many times these pups are returned to us as they reach maturity of size (not of mind) because they are growling, threatening to bite or becoming unruly. It often reminds me of my nieces and nephews. It's a good thing that they are not returnable for the same behaviours for which dogs get returned. I distinctly remember being bitten at least once by each of my little relatives and being snapped at multiple times, especially during their teenage years (and talk about being growly and rambunctious – some of them are still that way!) Still, I don't recall any attempts to return the children "because they will not have a child that bites." No, as I recall, the relatives settled into a training schedule which was proven to discourage this bad behaviour (no one said that the little brat should be "put down" – at least not that I recall. If they had, surely I would have stepped in to the rescue – don't you think?) And manners - none of the children was expected to come with good manners – as I recall, the parents worked hard at teaching those, too. Then they sent the little darlin's to school to learn the ways of the world.

Please allow me to state the obvious here. Those little relatives are at the top of the intelligence scale in this world, amazingly, but even then the parents invested hours and hours and years and years into teaching them to behave properly (some with varied success!) So, then, people obtain a puppy or dog and when it shows the same types of behaviours that our own youngsters do, we become all up at arms and proclaim that "we won't have a dog that bites" and feel compelled to kill it! That's often without even knowing that the behaviours can be managed, just like kids' behaviour. Let's see - teach the kids but expect the dog to come all trained . . . I have an option for you! Let's train them! Sort of like we do for our own (more intelligent) children who show the same behaviours! It's a wild idea, I know!

My own opinion is that every dog should go to a good obedience class with his guardian. It does so much good in so many ways, both for you and the dog. Obedience classes help you interact with your dog in ways that the dog can understand. With the differences in our body languages, the message you are trying to give to your dog may be the exact opposite of the message that your dog is actually receiving. The classes teach you to communicate with your dog, to socialize your dog with other people, other situations and other dogs. He learns that no matter where he is, he must look to you for guidance and obey as asked. Your dog becomes confident as he learns the ways of the world and to understand your requests. An obedience-trained dog is a happy, relaxed dog with many necessary and enjoyable social skills. (Oh, sort of like my nieces!)

There are many sites on the internet, too, which will help with some behaviour problems of cats or dogs. (Please, even if your intentions are good, do not bring your cat to obedience classes!) The help you need for your cat can be found on one of many sites. Also, many dog issues are addressed on these sites – things like food guarding and barking.

My favorite sites include *www.drsophiayin.com*, a site by a top veterinary behaviourist who leaves excellent tips on her blog and has many articles available (under "Recent Articles") addressing house training and dog bite prevention as well as many videos on such topics as training your dog to allow toenail trims. The ASPCA also has an excellent site with a "Pet Care" section with information on everything from travelling to feeding, allergies, weight loss and bad breath as well as training tips which are very useful. The resource library at *www.bestfriends.org* houses articles on rescuing, looking after almost any type of pet, as well as health care and training and approaches to use when trying to convince people to spay and neuter. This site is amazing, dealing as well with pet loss, emergencies, and chronicling the stories of rescued animals, including the Michael Vicks pit bulls which were rehabilitated there.

Other good sites for animal lovers interested in training and bettering the lives of animals include *www.animalbehaviourcollege.com*, *www.dogsdeservebetter.com*, the Canadian Federation of Humane Societies, the Humane Society of the United States and the National Humane Education Society.

The resources are there, whether on line or at obedience classes for dogs, especially for those with behaviour issues. The information is out there, books are everywhere, (One of my favourite dog management book is "The Dog Listener" by Jan Fennel which is available at Amazon – I highly recommend it!)

Armed with all the information and assistance out there, including behaviour assessments with your vet, dog behaviour can be modified and shaped so that your dog becomes the person that you want him to be – just like my relatives did! Well, sort of.

Cats, too, sort of. (They are more like my relatives – but I won't go there.) Still, cat behaviours can be molded and shaped into acceptable room-mate behaviour. These sites have excellent tips and instructions. Before you give up on your friend, take a tip from me and try some of these ideas.

PET LOSS

So often after losing their beloved pet, people will tell me that they will never get another dog. They will say that it hurts too much to lose them and that they don't want to go through that pain again. I agree – it does hurt to lose them. And it should! If you lose your best friend without a hiccough in your emotional well-being, perhaps the love was not mutual. The loss of a friend (human, canine or other) should hurt – that's how you know that you loved them. I understand too, the feeling of wanting to avoid the loss and grief when your pet passes.

But, think of this: that friend of yours gave you so much in the lifetime that he lived with you – unwavering love, comfort, caring, companionship, laughter and security. He gave you everything he had to give, with a little left over for your family and friends. The very fact that you feel so bereft at his passing tells me that you are an excellent dog guardian, that you care deeply for your friend and that he was safe and well cared for during the time that he was with you.

After a suitable period, in my book, you then top the list of prospective new adopters. You can never replace a special friend, we all know that – but you can make new friends! You can help another dog out there who, through no fault of his own, is homeless, and needs a loving family. It is not that they would be purposely bred so that you could get a new dog – they are out there anyway, and they need you! They need the love and caring that you have for dogs. They need the security and family that you can provide. This is in no way detrimental to the friend that you have lost. You know that your good friend would want you to care for another of his species and receive the enjoyment and well-being that comes from being with good friends. They are out there, waiting and wishing that they could be warm and secure, with someone that they love. They need people who care deeply. They need to be someone's dog.

It's funny that as I was trying to write this article, a friend e-mailed the following to me – I feel somewhat redundant and totally outclassed as I read this:

A DOG'S LAST WILL AND TESTAMENT

Before humans die, they write their Last Will and Testament, give their home and all they have to those they leave behind. If, with my paws, I could do the same, this is what I'd ask...

To a poor and lonely stray I'd give:

my happy home;
my bowl and cozy bed, soft pillows and all my toys;
the lap, which I loved so much;
the hand that stroked my fur and the
sweet voice which spoke my name.

I'd will to the sad, scared shelter dog, the place I had in my human's loving heart, of which there seemed no bounds.

So, when I die, please do not say, "I will never have a pet again, for the loss and pain is more than I can stand." Instead, go find an unloved dog, one whose life has held no joy or hope and give *my* place to *him*.

This is the only thing I can give . . . the love I left behind

~ Author Unknown

MAKE IT ALL WELL FOR YOUR DOG

I get such a kick out of the dogs here. Not one is the same and it is so easy to see what they are thinking – those of them that do think.

Take Ike, for instance. At fifteen years old and blind, you'd think he would not have much of a life, but let the doorbell ring and he'll show you how he enjoys his life. Having spent the entire day playing musical beds in various parts of the house, and quietly ignoring my entreaties to go out at least once (he must have to "go!") he's on his feet in a heartbeat and waiting for the visitor at the door. His tail wags that entire end of him and he oozes welcome and goodwill. He leans on his visitors and for the most part, they follow my instructions to greet him with familiarity and enthusiasm. Following the overwhelming excitement of the visit, he then retires for a well-deserved rest.

Today was packed with excitement for the whole pack – new, very large chewies were distributed to them. Everyone is excited to receive such a great treat. Ike joins in the noisy chewing with much enthusiasm, then after a few delicious moments, forgets about his prize and falls asleep. Call me evil, but I wake him up and present him with the same chewie. Again the "Oh, wow! A chewie!" response, followed by animated chewing and then a nap. Again, to my embarrassment, I awaken the old codger and again present the prize. Again comes the "Wow! A new chewie!" and renewed chewing, culminating in a nap. Aware that this could continue indefinitely, and exercising iron self control, I let him sleep and put his chewie in the drawer so that the others cannot take it. I wonder, "If he remembers this, will he think he was given four chewies today?" By my calculation, and assuming no other dog confiscates his prize, this one huge rawhide should satisfy Ike's daily chewing needs for about twenty seven weeks, given his speed and vigor at macerating it. Jerry, the shepherd has already demolished nine inches of his chewie and is eying Ike's with wolfish interest. Ike's, on the other hand is soggy on one end and the tip has been bent and deformed by the force of his chewing.

Then, there was the ball game, earlier in the day. Five dogs, three balls, (Seven, the husky, does not retrieve, and Hogan has other things on his mind) and a long downhill road. It is difficult getting started, almost impossible to throw the three balls at the same time, but once we get going, it is easy. Someone always has a ball at hand – grab it from the dog and throw. The down-hill road gives my throw a much greater distance, as does the bounce on the hard frozen surface. So Miles, the border collie mix brings his ball back and stands up, putting the ball in my hands – I love that, it's so easy. Then comes Dreyfus, sliding into me and almost knocking me off my feet. He will never let go of the ball and I'm so tired of those tugging matches that can sometimes last for several minutes. Fortunately, I've found that he has a release latch at the lower right corner of his jaw, just under his ear. Grab that, hold on and the mouth opens, releasing the ball. This has made games so much easier since I found that ball release latch. Who knew that thing was there?

Next comes Jerry – he's all about getting the ball, so the minute I murmur "Give," Jer drops it at my feet. His most fervent wish is that he be allowed to retrieve it again - and again. Pick it up and throw quickly before Hogan, side-swipes me, while trying to keep all the dogs in one close herd. He's so focused on the group that he has no interest in the balls. He has already run three times the distance the others have, in his attempts to keep the canine herd together, and looks so proud when all the dogs get into the back of my small car ahead of him. He's finally corralled them, and feels that he has put in a good day's work. His gaze meets mine in awareness of a job well done. Good boy, Hogan!

Tonight, there will be no restless pacing, no unnecessary and irritating demands to go outside repeatedly. Tonight, the pack will rest quietly and contentedly. Their exercise needs have been met, they have had a good chewing session and they are with their human and canine pack members. It is as it should be in their world. All is well.

RANDALL

Here's what we know about Randall:

> We know Randall has been seen in a community near Grand Falls for the past six or seven years.
>
> We know that he was considered a "community cat" (a stray), and that some residents made sure that he was fed and had shelter.
>
> We know that, although he gratefully accepted the food, he could not bring himself to accept the warmth of their homes.
>
> We know that sometime in the past several weeks Randall suffered a devastating injury – either by an animal attack or perhaps a traffic accident – maybe a snow plow injury.

We know that Randall fought for several weeks, through severe pain and hunger, and we know that he finally, in desperation, went to someone and asked for help.

We know that Randall made an excellent choice when he chose to drag his crippled body through the newly-fallen snow to the home of his rescuer, leaving a broad trail in his wake.

We also know that person drove him for an hour to find the medical attention that he so desperately needed.

We know that Randall's severe injuries led to chronic infections in his sides and back, and that the damage to his back has affected his ability to walk.

As vets, we know that Randall's injuries will leave him, always, slow and lame, unable to survive outdoors.

We know that his back and his abilities will never be the same.

We know that our drugs, antibiotics and laser treatments will help to heal and subdue the pain that this big orange tomcat has suffered with for so long.

We know that we can help him back to the point where he can enjoy life once again.

We know and are awed by the fact that this timid cat made a conscious decision to ask for help.

We know that he made the right choice and we know that we are honoured to be able to help him.

We know all that – but here's what we don't know.

We don't know where that little guy got the strength to survive those horrible wounds.

We don't know how he found the courage to ask for help from the very people that he had avoided for so many years.

We don't know where he got the wisdom to choose the right person.

We don't know where he got the courage to allow total strangers to care for his wounds and manage his recovery.

And, visiting him in his kennel where he is rapidly healing and getting stronger every day, we don't know how this little orange tomcat, this loner, can be so full of love, so accepting of visitors and so happy to receive a gentle pat, return a head butt and accept the admiration of his visitors.

No, we don't know where he got the strength, the determination, the courage, the wisdom and the love.

Or do we?

WORLD SPAY DAY

World Spay Day was started in 1995, and originally focussed on the need to spay and neuter feral cats. It is now a world-wide event focussing on eliminating pet overpopulation everywhere. Spaying females and neutering males is a 100% effective method of contraception in dogs and cats. By preventing unwanted litters of puppies and kittens, we decrease the number of animals living in dangerous situations or ending up in shelters, where they are often killed as a way of dealing with their numbers. We stop the unnecessary suffering of neglected, frozen, starving, unwanted excess cats. This is a world-wide problem with a very simple answer – say it after me: "I'm into S & N" (spay and neuter). If some Bristol residents had spayed and neutered, the workload of one very kind and determined person would be lessened. (Her bills would also be decreased.)

The Bristol Ferals were recently the recipients of the kindness of a local resident. Amanda noticed many ferals living in the community and made it her heart hurt. She became determined to ensure they were spayed and neutered (so that they didn't perpetuate the problem) and fed and given warm shelter. She will continue to work to find them safe homes. Amanda took on this huge project because she believes that it is wrong to leave these creatures, the result of our careless disregard for their lives and the welfare of their descendants. One or two spays done years ago could have prevented this colony from reaching the size that Amanda is dealing with now. Please visit Bristol's Strays on Facebook to see her ongoing efforts. We're proud to be associated with her and are grateful that she's taken on this task to help strays, raise awareness and educate our community on their ongoing plight. It's a problem of society, and it will take society to make a change. Amanda has started the process in Bristol and is now looking for homes for these fortunate animals. Sadly, the beautiful big white tom whom she had named Braveheart was struck and killed before he could be live-trapped. This is the misfortune of too many. Come on, Bristol – help Amanda! Get into spays and neuters!

THE QUEEN OF SPAYEDS

They call us the Queens of Spayeds
We fix them, in all their shades
Black, white, grey and yellow
We fix them all and make them mellow
They call us the Queens of Spayeds

It all started with no fanfare
We fixed them for their welfare
Shocked to see there were so many
We fixed 'em so they won't have any
That's why we're the Queens of Spades

Some say that they're not broken
Sadder words were never spoken
Now so many live on the street
Fearing everything they meet
We worry, the Queens of Spades

Until Each One Has a Home

We see them most every day
Hurt in the most awful way
Or surviving for many a week
Before finding the aid they seek
We're angry! The Queens of Spayeds

Volunteer to help the strays
Evenings, weekends, any days
This world needs no more kittens
They'll lose more than just their mittens
We'll all be the Queens of Spayeds

They are out there, they have no homes
They're living- not garden gnomes
They struggle, they need a hand
All this breeding should be banned!
Let's all be the Queens of Spayeds

So, ladies, I'm asking you
There is more we all can do!
We don't need more cats to suffer
Let's all act, let's be their buffer
Let's all be The Queens of Spayeds

SEVEN

Last weekend, a free spirit floated free one final time! My blue-eyed friend, Seven, the husky, died suddenly, with no warning. There is a gaping hole in my life and in the pack.

Where is that pup who, when she first came here, was so cute that she looked like a stuffed toy? Where is the instigator of games, the hoarder of toys, the digger of the deepest holes, the escape artist extraordinaire? Who will lay their head on my lap and, with the most sincere expression, the most loving gaze, declare her life-long and everlasting love for me, and then give an identical repeat performance to the virtual stranger across the room from me? Who will "Wooooo" when I reach for the dog treat package and then sneakily try to steal the blind dog's treat? Who will keep my back warm at night - and then growl each time I dare to move? Who will now steal the food from the cupboard and chew my favourite gloves?

No longer will I have to drive up and down the local streets, looking for the Houdini who, this time, climbed a tree to jump over the fence. No longer will I be driving, worriedly, past my neighbour's houses, shouting "Seven!" (At least I didn't name her "Four!")

Just that morning, we had played Bedmice (you know, you move your hand under the blankets and she tries to catch the "mice"), and I laughed out loud at the eleven-year-old pup that she was, enjoying her laughing eyes and that big grin.

Who will teach the foster pups to respect their elders? Who will strike fear in the hearts of any dog who tries to take her toys or to sleep in her bed? Who will take care of any boo-boos that might happen to the others in the pack? Who will tire of watching the ball dogs search fruitlessly for the lost ball, before showing them – "It's right there, Stupid!"

And who will charm every acquaintance, teacher, student, trainer or vet staff with their endless goodness and love – and run away from home, just to be with others?

No one. That personality can never be replaced! That "Seven of Nine" of mine. I can't help but wonder: How will they keep her at Rainbow Bridge? Do they have high fences?

YOUR DONATIONS AT WORK

Dear DunRoamin' Supporter

Over the past few weeks, we have spent quite a bit of the money that you kindly donated to our strays. Oh, not for kitty litter or food - we have had a windfall of that donated over the Christmas season, much to our relief. No, we spent some of your donations on the rescued strays that came to us. I thought that you might be interested in seeing examples of how your money is spent, so have chosen to review the last few emergencies that we have received.

We applied some of your monetary donations and many of your blankets and towels in the treatment and care of a young dog found unconscious and lying in the snow on the side of the highway. She was so cold that her temperature did not register on our thermometer (normal temperature is thirty-eight point five degrees Celcius, and the lowest reading on our thermometer is thirty-two degrees.) Only the very slow, intermittent, slight rise and fall of her chest indicated that she was still alive. After many hours of warming her to normal body temperature, giving IV therapy and treating her shock and pain, she got to her feet, limped her tiny bruised body across the room and applied her "Save a starving dog" expression to her very impressionable vet. With a full stomach, warm and safe, pain treated, she curled into a ball and slept the sleep of the exhausted. She is now in a foster home doing very well and your donations will help with the costs of her spay and vaccinations. The little tramp is okay now, and almost finished her heat cycle. We call her Norma Jean.

Another emergency almost caused an international incident. The tiny, thin cat travelled from Bath, NB to Houlton, Maine on the undercarriage of a car. Thankfully, the driver heard her crying and mechanics were able to remove her from her dangerous and icy perch. She'd climbed up under the motor, as many cats do in the winter, searching for a little warmth from the engine. It is so cold out there if you are homeless. It's a wonder that "Crankshaft" wasn't killed! The trials and tribulations of her life were very evident in her frail, thin body and in her traumatically amputated tail (that looked to be about a week old.) Her eyes darted in all directions, her demeanour very frightened. Your donations supported this little survivor over the shock period and helped with the costs of pain medications and antibiotics. When she is well enough, they will also help with the costs of vaccinations, testing for feline leukemia and feline AIDS and in her spay and tail repair. As she heals and learns to trust, she's not nearly as "Cranky" as originally thought. She knows that, although she almost got the shaft, she's okay now.

Then there was the very sick young tabby cat abandoned by her family and caught by some caring neighbours - and none too soon, judging by the difficulties that she was having, just to breathe. She's a very friendly, cuddly little thing, now that she knows that she will not be harmed. She was just so confused and frightened at being abandoned like that while she was so sick and the weather was so cold. Your help allowed us to treat her with IV therapy, antibiotics, special foods and some anti-viral medications. We desperately hoped that she could rally, and rally she did! When she is well enough, she, too, will be tested for the feline viruses, vaccinated and spayed, thanks to your donations. Then, Rally will be ready for a good home.

These lovely animals are just a few of those who have recovered and will move on to better, safer homes and will not contribute offspring to the dangerous world from which they came. Your help was essential in their survival and recoveries. Your help is essential in stopping the reproduction of unwanted animals in a world where there are so many desperate for homes. They are grateful, DunRoamin' is grateful, staff is grateful, volunteers are grateful, animal lovers and advocates are grateful. It's all about the animals, and if you could see one of them, you'd see "Grateful" personified.

Thank you for all your support. Without you, what would have happened to all these wonderful little guys - the "four-legged folk" who still need our help?

YOU GOTTA CARE

People of note have been inspiring us to be the best that we can be, to get passionate about something, to try to make a difference where we can. So often people say that they would love to help, but just can't find the time. (I'm not talking only about DunRoamin', right now. We do what we do because this is something about which we are passionate, and we have the skills to help.) There are so many areas where you can make a difference, where your skills - be it compassion, interest in gardening, love for the elderly, interest in children, ability to teach reading skills, writing, skateboarding, dancing or horseback riding - will help someone somewhere, with improving their confidence, increasing feelings of self worth, lessening loneliness, or opening new doors to increase someone's belief in their own capabilities. Not only will that person be helped, but the emotional and spiritual rewards that you, the giver, will reap will surprise you.

Someone once said, "And can it be that in a world so full and busy, that the loss of one weak creature makes a void in my heart so deep and wide that nothing but the width and depth of eternity can ever fill it up." The person whose world was so full and busy was Charles Dickens. In his time, he too, thought that life was very busy. It is relative. But he also noted the worth of others and the fact that he cared deeply about them.

Another inspirational quote which parallels the starfish quote that we use "I made a difference for that one," was Edmund Burke who said, "No one could make a greater mistake than he who did nothing because he could only do a little." What seems like "a little" to you might mean everything to the recipient of that little gift. The smallest kindness has been known to change a stranger's mind about committing suicide. How's that for a "little" thing?

According to Oscar Wilde, "The smallest act of kindness is worth more than the grandest of intentions." I take his point to be, don't just sit there, do whatever you can to make the world a better place, no matter who or what the improvements benefit. Intentions do nothing. Action is necessary to make a difference. To miss out on the feeling of accomplishment and pride that I feel when one of our previously dying strays is adopted, healthy, into a great home, is not worth the sleep that I would have had if I didn't help, or the money that would be in my pocket, but for the donations to help the strays. This is an addictive feeling, one that I wouldn't miss for the world.

And George Bernard Shaw said, "The worst sin toward our fellow creatures is not to hate them, but to be indifferent to them. That is the essence of inhumanity." At least they must be acknowledged to be hated. To be indifferent means that you cannot see them and that caring is not present. Looking into the eyes of any of our strays and not feeling anything seems to be an impossibility for me. I wonder what they must be thinking, how they felt on realizing that they were abandoned, or that a cruelty had just been inflicted on them. I wonder what they must think when some caring person warms them, feeds them and finds help for them. It seems that it must be more simple for animals, their understanding of your aid more "in the moment." Certainly helping animals is not as complicated as helping people – but not more important.

Then, a great philosopher of our time said, in his work, The Lorax, "Unless someone like you cares a whole awful lot. Things aren't going to get better, they're *not*!" For many of us, Dr. Seuss has been a big presence in our lives and his words carry much weight.

So, whether you can do a little or a lot, for animals, for your community, for children, for the elderly, the poor, the lonely, the neighbours or the troubled, the important thing is that you *do* it. You never know when, what you consider a small thing, a small kindness, may make an important contribution to someone's wellness and have far-reaching effects. You can be a hero to someone without ever knowing it. All you need to do is care and be kind and helpful.

Another favorite quote of mine, which, in a way, fits with DunRoamin's starfish theme, is one by Nelson Rockefeller who said, "You can't leave footprints in the sands of time while sitting down!"

Mildred A. Drost DVM

I don't know where this article came from, it certainly isn't like me to wax philosophical, but I think there are some good points here. Try it - you'll like it, that feeling of having made a difference to someone or something.

Yes, I know – the voices in my head may not be real – but they have some good ideas sometimes!

PRESS 1

Due to the large numbers of calls that DunRoamin' has been receiving, and to try to meet the many and varied needs of those who contact DunRoamin' for help, we have opened an automated system to direct your inquiries to the person most likely to be of assistance. Please choose, from the following list of options, the situation that most closely describes yours.

> If your dog has nine pups and you want us to take them all, press 1.
>
> If you have had your cats for ten years, are now expecting a baby and want to be rid of the cats, press 2.
>
> If you have found a kitten, and if we don't take it you will "take care of it," press 3.

If the town wants your dog gone because kids in the area are always teasing it and it is becoming aggressive, press 4.

If you want us to take your six-year old dog because it barks, is itchy and its medications cost fifteen dollars a month, press 5.

If you have twenty cats – mothers and their kittens, and you are going to college and want us to take all your cats, press 6.

If you have had your cat for three or four months and will adopt him if DunRoamin' pays for his neuter, press 7.

If you declined our offer to pay half of the spay fee for your cat last year and now have that cat and her three daughters, all with litters of kittens now, and want us to take all of them, press 8.

If you want your two pit bulls spayed and you'd like us to pick them up, spay them at no cost to you and return them, press 9.

If you have noticed three tiny kittens in the ditch in the pouring rain for the last three days and think someone should do something, press 10.

If you have five dogs, live an hour away from us, can't afford to feed them and would like us to deliver dog food, press 11.

If a dog is chasing your chickens, press 12.

If you will throw your house cat outside in the snow if we won't take it, press 13.

If you would like to adopt one of our dogs, one who doesn't shed, doesn't bark and does not run away when left outside, press 14.

If other dogs come into your yard and breed your female dogs, and this is your fifth unwanted litter in two years, and you don't want the pups in your house, press 15.

If you took in a stray kitten several months ago and want DunRoamin' to "fix it" at no charge or you are not interested in keeping the cat, press 16.

If you have a stray female cat in cat breeding season and you want us to take her, but only if we promise not to spay her because you don't believe in abortion, but she cannot come inside, press 17.

If your son wants one of our dogs and you want to know if you can use a shock collar on it if he gets one, press 18.

If you have a lot of cats and are on a fixed income and would like us to continually supply you with a specific brand of cat food, press 19.

If you don't like our tone and attitude when we ask questions to try to sort calls out in a manner favourable to the animals, press 20.

Mildred A. Drost DVM

If you have found a sick or badly-injured stray that needs immediate and expensive veterinary care, and will bring the victim to the clinic, call me immediately. I will do anything for those poor little lost waifs who have no one to look after them or speak for them.

JERRY

I think my rescued Shepherd Jerry has a foot fetish! He is always lying on my feet and always carries my footwear around with him, just laying it on the floor beside him as he sleeps, but then picking it up to carry with him as he moves to another spot. It is annoying, in a way, as I'm always wandering around the house with the chosen footwear on one foot, unable to find neither hide nor hair of the other one. (Actually, did you recognize the pun there, most footwear being made of leather, but it was the "hair" part that made me smile. I found lots of that, to my chagrin, and I just vacuumed yesterday! No shoe, though – it was out in the yard!) But, to my point, what is it about my shoes that he finds so attractive - my clothing, jackets, gloves, et cetera, being equally available? Also, why am I spending all that money on toys for him if he is only interested in my shoes? I guess I could minimize his belongings if I could just get a handle on the launching and trajectory of the thrown shoe verses the thrown ball. Somehow I think that if, all else being equal, shoes could be launched with the same effectiveness as balls, my dogs' favourite sport would be "shoe" instead of "ball." Yes, I think that someone far wiser than I am has already figured that out.

So, then, why? My shoes? Really, though, I know he doesn't have a foot fetish! First of all he's a dog, and secondly, I did his surgery when I adopted him. He doesn't care about that stuff!

You know what I think? After thinking this thing through, I have concluded that Jerry carries my shoes because he is my boy and he knows it. And I am his as well, and my scent is comforting to him. He likes to have it close by. His devotion is flattering, in a way. He's such a nice dog!

No, that can't be it! Even I can smell some of my footwear, especially my walking shoes. Why would he, an amazing creature whose nose can pick up the scent of one particle of accelerant in a room burned by an arsonist, need to bring my footwear with him to smell my odor? He can probably smell my feet when I turn into my driveway, especially after a busy day at work!

Now that I think about this more carefully, I realize that my other belongings aren't as easily available to Jerry. His eye level is much lower than mine. He would be much more likely to notice a shoe on the floor, as opposed to my clothing on the dresser or stuffed into a laundry hamper. Yes, that's it. Oh, and I do leave my footwear scattered around the house. I could stop him just by putting my shoes in the closet! It would be that easy.

They say that each dog comes into your life for a reason. If that is the case, then Jerry must be a multi-tasker. He must have come into my life to teach me tolerance, to strengthen my throwing arm, and to prove that appearance is just appearance. Also, Jerry must be here to teach me to understand the concept of patience (versus "patients," which I should already have a handle on), to appreciate natural beauty, and to recognize "goodness" when I see it. Or maybe he came to teach me to be neat. Shoes are expensive!

Still, I like to believe Jerry does it to show his love for me. I can't put an end to that, can I? Ooh! Thinking of that super-duper, extra heavy duty nose that he has, and the over powering scent that must come from my sneakers . . . poor Jerry!! What that dog goes through for me!!!

THINGS

I thought that I would write today about some of the things that have made me smile this week. There are so many negative occurrences that we've found a way to make many negatives into positives. When I was a nurse, this was called black humour. At DunRoamin', I think it is called stress reduction and mental survival. (And, yes, I admit to having a warped mind, but it keeps me sane.)

My first giggle of the week occurred when I left a prescription for one of our rescued dogs on the answering machine at our local pharmacy. When I dropped in at the drugstore to pick up the medication, I met with a somewhat concerned pharmacist, who, aware that we had had hawks, coyotes and foxes in the clinic, wondered at our sanity in taking on a moose. We had a chuckle as I realized that I had been remiss in designating "species" while reciting my prescription. "Moose" is the name of our delightful new canine patient, and a relieved pharmacist concurred with my drug dosage as well, since a moose would require much more drug than I had ordered. "Well," she said, "I have a horse on medication from here and several dogs and cats, so…"

Later in the week, Martha, my sister and strong supporter of Dun Roamin' got a text from Dr Monteith informing her that an employee had seen a black and white cat jumping out of the dumpster when she took the garbage out. The cat was now lodged in the tight space under our storage building. As she read the text, Martha was aware of the unspoken part: "And it's cold, raining, wet and she's a drop-off, scared and probably hungry … "

When we arrived at the crisis site, Dr Monteith had all four sides of the building blocked with various bits and pieces of lumber and equipment from the builders. She was unable to reach the cat but had seen that she was extremely thin. No one could, in good conscience, leave her there and go to our warm homes. Bravely, Dr Monteith and I lay in the cold mud to peer under the shed. Eventually we spotted her hiding behind the one brick under the entire building. We discussed our options and armed with two long boards and a salmon net, we again lay in the cold mud. My job was to encourage her to move to the other side of the space which gave more room for the salmon net to move. We had named her Effie Trinket (from the movie "Hunger Games") by this point, but, after a time, her name seemed to get mis-pronounced more often than not! I won't bore you with details of the hunt; suffice it to say that by the end we had a small crowd of onlookers, including my sister, the foster mother of one of our dogs, the clinic book-keeper and a sales person for a prescription pet food company. Although warm and dry, they all seemed to have better ideas for catching the cat than we did. The end was anticlimactic, with the cat suddenly walking over to the area of the net where Dr Monteith deftly lifted it and allowed it to settle over the cat's head. She was, "Like, let's get it over with!" She was pulled into the open and the net twisted to prevent her escape and we quickly retreated to the warmth of the clinic.

Inside, she was removed carefully from her trap and immediately sighed and began purring and kneading. See, that's the thing with cats – she could have saved us all that wallowing in the mud and gravel if she had just let us know that she was tame. Instead, she seemed put off by the mud on my clothing, preferring to sit on a clean person. Nonetheless, she was very thin and required treatment for a severe ulcer in her mouth that affected her ability to eat. She's back in our good graces now though, having had the decency to respond to Dr Monteith's treatment and at least is beginning to gain some weight. Little Effie Trinket will soon be ready for a new, and better, home.

The other thing that made me laugh, if only a bit bitterly, was when a staff member found a box containing tiny kittens on the clinic doorstep in the middle of a work day. Someone didn't even come inside to speak for them, just dumped and left. They did, however, leave a note saying that they "knew how busy we were," but nonetheless, left us with four more little unwanted kittens to add to our already impressive collection of desperate orphans. It is only through the resilience of the young, (here I mean vet techs, assistants and summer students) that they are able to get up multiple times through the night to attend to these little guys and still arrive at work in the morning ready to do their jobs. They're good! I hardly ever have to wake them up to get them to work with me.

This article just speaks to the commitment of our volunteers and our learned ability to overlook the people who have treated these animals in these ways. There is no point in wasting energy being angry. We'll just keep on trying to get through to people. A simple spay and neuter of someone's pet would have prevented all the suffering of the kittens and volunteer caregivers and prevented the mud-stains on our clothes.

GOODBYE IKE

Maybe you've noticed on the DunRoamin' Memorials Page that we lost Ike, the very old blind rescue dog, a few weeks ago. His quality of life had rapidly deteriorated in the preceding week until finally I knew he was ready to go.

I miss him, but am getting a more restful night's sleep now. Ike, like many old people, had become forgetful and needed extra assistance, especially at night. He started by barking in the middle of the night, in his own inimitable way: "Wow, Wow," then silence, then, "Wow, Wow," then silence. At first, I thought that I had forgotten to lead him into the bedroom with all the others when I went to bed. Then, the next night I realized that, although I had led him in to bed, he was now in the kitchen. I'm not proud of this, but at his first few episodes of this barking in the middle of the night, I tried to avoid getting out of bed for him. He knew the house like the back of his paw and he knew very well that at this time of night, I was tucked into my bed. Since he came here, I have tried to make a routine for him, especially at night. Still, "Wow! Wow!"

"I'm in the bedroom, Ike!" Silence. I'm almost asleep, then "Wow! Wow!"

"IKE! I'M IN THE BEDROOM!" Silence. "Wow! Wow!"

"IKE! I'M IN THE BEDROOM! YOU KNOW! I GO HERE EVERY NIGHT! IT'S WHERE WE SLEEP! YOU KNOW HOW TO COME WITH ME!" Silence. Then, "Wow! Wow!"

"IIIKKEE!!! WE'RE IN THE BEEDDRROOMM!! JUST LIKE ALWAYS!!" Silence. "Wow! Wow!"

"COME OONNN, IKE JUST WALK INTO THE HALL AND TURN RIGHT. I'M RIGHT THERE!!"

"Wow! Wow!"

"OK, I'll come and get you. C'mon, you old fool, let's go to bed! COME ON, IKE! Why won't you come with me? DO YOU NEED TO GO OUT?"

A stampede of large dogs flows through the living room, sweeping Ike and me along with it and out into the run. The others leave the deck and do what they need to do, but Ike shuffles to the rail and urinates over the side. Well, he's not the only old male who has done that! I turn him and he is swept into the house by the other dogs, and I use this momentum to direct him into the bedroom.

"Okay, buddy, here's your bed, I'm right here, Let's go to sleep." A half hour later – "Wow! Wow!"

"Ike! I'm right here, big guy!" I place my hand on his head and soon feel him settling. His panting gradually slows and he falls asleep. I return my now numb arm and hand to the bed and fall a sleep again. The next day, I hear the same bark, from the pen. The door is opened. He always comes in by himself. I look out. He has his back to the deck and seems lost. I call, "Ike! Up here!" With obvious relief he turns toward my voice and follows the sound that I make by slapping my hand on my leg. The vet in me begins to clue in – the dog is confused and frightened. I congratulate myself on my handling of his fear the previous night! My voice is a bit hoarse from all that yelling. I feel two inches tall.

This was the beginning of the downhill slide, and within a few short weeks he was gone. I was glad that I had had the "Duh" moment when I realized that he was confused and frightened. With a little extra care, we were able to keep him grounded by making sure that he was with me or settled sleeping next to Jerry, who is the only dog who doesn't become offended if Ike sleeps on his bed too, or accidentally steps on him.

Now, Ike's gone. His ashes are in the closet with all the rest – Dixon, Seven, Bogart, and ten or twelve more.

Then, a good friend called to talk about Ike's loss and started my thoughts in a whole new direction. She knows that my closet is the storage place for the cremains of perhaps fifteen to seventeen dogs, dating back to vet school and on to the present. "Well," she commented, "I hope your house never burns down when you are not around. Imagine the poor crime scene people when they find seventeen different types of DNA in that one spot in what was surely a closet." And the speculation: "She must have been a hoarder who kept seventeen dogs in that one closet. Those poor dogs -crammed into that one little area! How could she?!?"

Well, my friend, I think that this little exposé has put a stop to those types of rumours. Sure, I don't mind being "the crazy dog lady." My family is already blessed with a "crazy cat lady." Maybe we could pool our craziness and see what happens. Oh, wait, we already did that, and the waves from that have swept in many others with similar tendencies. Now, we're swamped by wave after wave of crazy cats and kittens – the ones no one wants. Why is it that people continue making them when they don't even really want the one they have? I don't have any answers.

IT'S ALL ABOUT THE ANIMALS

If I could say just one thing to all the animal rescue, shelter and education groups out there and their employees and volunteers, it would be this: it is all about the animals! It is not a political platform. It is not about who is best. It is not about who lives where or where the fundraising is being done. It is not about your resume or your agenda. It is not about whether you agree with the board, the shelter manager or the supervising veterinarian's decisions. It is not about expectations of having an "in" that allows you to have your own pets spayed or neutered at a discounted rate. It is not about you. It *is* all about what is best for the animals. That's it. That's all.

Often in the office, people will tell me, "I adopted him from the shelter," feeling guilty that the animal didn't come from DunRoamin'. But I think that's great! These animals all need homes, no matter where they originated. As long as people are not perpetuating the suffering of puppy mill dogs by buying the pups, I am always happy for the animal, whether he/she is a familiar DunRoamin' pet, one from a shelter, or a stray that has been rescued by a family. They all need homes and a safe caring environment where their lives are not continuously in danger or where they are not constantly reproducing.

If a genie magically appeared before me, from the old lamp that I still use in my living room, I could easily supply three wishes without any need to think about it for a second:

- let there be more compassion for animals and more consideration for their suffering in the general population;
- let more people understand the necessity of spaying and neutering their pets; and
- let the animal care workers do their jobs well, with compassion for man and animal alike, with pure motives aimed at improving the lives of animals and people alike and let those people whose choice it is to work for the betterment of those animal lives, work together in harmony, not in competition with each other.

The tongue can be a powerful weapon and can sway opinions easily if comments are repeated loudly and often enough. The result is too often to the detriment of the animals. If your opinion does not click with certain policies of your animal shelter, perhaps you do not completely understand the reasons for policy implementation. Perhaps there are municipal or medical reasons for the decisions that have been made.

People bashing, regardless of your position, is never productive. If tempted to complain aloud, workers should consider, "How will this help the animals?" In my opinion the answer is, "It won't!" Constructive dialogue helps. We should all remember that it is always about the animals, and rather than complain about individual quirks that people have, we should celebrate the fact that these people are committed to addressing the deficiencies in our society's treatment of pets.

THE SAD LOSS OF A WONDERFUL PET

Someone's young female cat died last night. The little grey tabby was found struggling on the side of the road over twenty-four hours previously. Good Samaritans helped her and brought her directly to DunRoamin'. We know that she was someone's pet because her coat was beautiful and shiny and she was a little overweight.

She was not frightened and accepted us immediately. I wonder if her family knew she was pregnant. Her injuries were such that we knew that she might not make it. We did everything that we could to assist in her fight to survive and to make her as comfortable as possible. She was so sweet and loving. Despite having an IV inserted and several injections of anti-shock drugs, antibiotics and pain medications, she was never aggressive. She made no attempts to scratch or bite. She accepted her treatments as if she understood the reasons for them. She held no grudges.

Yesterday morning, we felt that her condition had deteriorated. There was nothing more that we could do medically. We all said a prayer for her.

We had hoped desperately that she could hold on and recover from her terrible injuries but that was not to be. Last night, with her new friends at her side, she left this world and went to Rainbow Bridge.

Such a short life! If only she hadn't been on the road!

ADOPTING DREYFUS

Well, after fostering and enjoying my friend Dreyfus for almost two years, I've decided that I should keep him. I had been looking for the place where Dreyfus could get more attention than one-eighth of the time that I have available. He thrives on attention and is the only dog I've ever known who can interact with people at DunRoamin' events for the entire day without becoming exhausted. I am used to going home for a fresh dog halfway through longer events, like the day-long yard sale. Dreyf was still looking for more attention as we were packing up to go home, having been the centre of many interested and admiring cliques of children and adults for the entire day. His kennel mate, Moose, had packed up and gone home, exhausted, hours before.

So, I had a little chat with Dreyf the other night. I thought that I should officially inform him of my decision to adopt him and keep him here with me. I said, "Dreyf, you're adopted."

He looked at me quizzically as if to say, "Well, I never thought that you were my birth mother! We just look too different!"

Heartened, then, that the beginning seemed to have gone so well, I continued, "So you will be staying with me forever."

"Never planned on leaving!" said his eyes.

"No, Dreyf," I said, "I mean that you are officially my dog!"

"Always have been," he answered. "I signed the papers today," I told him.

"We don't need no papers to make it official!" was his response.

"See, Dreyf," I said, "I mean that you're not DunRoamin' anymore."

"I ben dun roamin for almost two years," his eyes told me as he cocked his head to one side, confused with our conversation.

"Yes, you have," I tried again. "But now you're mine!"

"Yap! Two years now," he replied.

"You don't get it do you?" I said.

"Didn't know you threw anything," he responded, glancing around for his ball. In desperation, I tried once more. "Dreyf, you're mine!"

"Yap," he replied, "and you're mine!"

It is going to be a long life with Dreyf. Not sure I did the smartest thing possible.

Having confessed all this, I guess it might be a good time to confess to another incident in Dreyfus' life. See, there was a time, when he first came to DunRoamin' that he was taken home by an older lady to see if he would get along with her dog and cats. She was in the middle of renovating her old farmhouse. In every way, it was a fiasco. I was called by the clinic the next morning to come to get him, as the lady had dropped him off at eight am, as he was "not suitable". She did not stay to discuss his unsuitability. Several days later, I had summoned enough nerve to call her to ask about his behaviour. Here's her story, to the best of my recollection.

Upon arriving at her house, Dreyfus immediately greeted her dog and marked every flower or otherwise raised area in her front yard. He was not aggressive to her dog, so was brought into the house. After a quick sniff of her house and a sort of distracted greeting of her dog, he immediately started jumping on the door, as if to go out. She allowed him out into her fenced backyard, where he immediately needed to come in. This went on for some time until, on one of his "in" episodes, he spotted her dainty little cat and immediately charged in that direction. Frightened, the cat bolted to the stairs and up to the spare bedroom where the lady had been applying paint. She had apparently left the lid of the paint can loose when she closed it. On one of his flying trips around the room in search of the cat, or perhaps on one of her trips evading him, somehow the can got knocked onto the new rug, leaving a markedly different pattern and colour in that one area. He was chastised, removed from the room and the paint was cleaned as well as possible. The carpet was turned to put the stained area under the bed.

She then left the room to find a rather large, well-formed but smelly deposit on the landing outside the bedroom door. This she picked up and deposited in the nearby toilet and flushed. She then watched in horror as the toilet blocked and water ran over its sides and onto her bathroom floor. A handy plunger remedied the blockage problem, but not before it had run across the bathroom floor and out into the hallway. Dreyfus and the cat watched in fascination as she wiped up the bathroom floor and then did a thorough scrub of the hallway.

Upon returning to the downstairs, she noted that her own dog was not in sight and found him in the den, having lifted and chewed a rather large area from the corner of the rug there. Some time was spent in rearranging the room to cover the newest damage. By this point, Dreyf and the cat had settled into an uneasy truce and she was frightened that one false move by any one of the three would start the games again. She was not about to take her eyes from any one of them. Her upset with Dreyfus and her own dog apparently fueled their nervous tendencies and both dogs paced and panted for the (short) remainder of the night, leaving them all awake very early the next morning and able to meet the clinic staff on their arrival for work.

I must say that I have never noted these tendencies in the big lug, but have endured my share of bruises and discomforts due to his behaviour. He has no idea that he is supposed to wait until the ball has left my hand before he grabs for it, and in that way has caused multiple inflammations and tendencies toward arthritis in my arms and shoulders. His size places his plume of a tail at the exact height to dust my coffee table and end tables; however, he makes no allowances for the personal items that may be on either. I should receive my new glasses next week and really hated that bite guard anyway.

Wish us luck. He'll stay with me as long as my nerves (and wallet) can take it.

TOO MANY PETS

Recently I was involved in assisting a gentleman who had helped several freezing and starving stray cats this past winter by sharing the warmth of his house and supplying food for them. As cats will do, these few multiplied over time this summer and now health officials had decided that the numbers must be drastically reduced. The man kept saying, "What could I do? I couldn't leave them out there to freeze." Many others had done that, but he couldn't. His conscience would not let him. Still, he was unable to afford the costs of the spays and neuters required by his rescues and ultimately we were called to see if we could help in some way.

Friends and family of this gentleman told us over and over how they had asked for help from the SPCA and were told that that group did not "do" stray cats. They had also called the shelters and were not given any help. Shelters do just that – they shelter animals. They do not have the resources or staff to trap and remove any stray animals, no matter how much the area might want it done. They struggle just to feed and look after (and treat and spay and neuter) the unwanted pets that are dropped on their doorstep. They have no time, equipment or energy to go out to other areas to pick up nuisance or stray, homeless animals that are struggling to survive on their own.

While I have difficulty accepting that our one official and legal entity for animal welfare and prevention of cruelty to animals, the NBSPCA, doesn't "do" cats, I think that much of the anger that I perceived from this gentleman and his family and friends would have been better directed, not at the hard-working shelters, but at the root cause of the huge problem that millions fight all across this country and the United States: the irresponsible pet owners who allow their animals to breed knowing that there are not enough homes out there for the animals already living. Why would they allow more to be born?

These owners who allow their pets to breed place an unfair physical burden and an unfair financial burden on people who have the caring and compassion to want to prevent the suffering of these poor unwanted individual animals. Yes, I know the next thought is that veterinary care is so expensive! Everything is! Yet these same people are able to smoke, drive big vehicles, take trips and enjoy expensive lifestyles. The blame cannot be placed at the feet of the veterinarians, either. It still goes right back to the owners who allow their animals to breed. That's it - that's the cause, right there.

My point in writing this is to remind people that the blame should be placed where it belongs – at the feet of any pet owner who allows their animals to breed. We don't need more pets! We need more responsible owners. We need owners who value the life placed in their care and who have the compassion to see that they, at least, will not add to this critical overpopulation problem.

BERNICE

I need to tell you about my newest favourite dog, Bernice. She is known to us at the clinic. We've been worrying about her for the last couple of years, and finally she was surrendered to DunRoamin' since she had acquired yet another massive face full of porcupine quills. (There is a way to prevent quills from happening. It's not a secret - keep your dog safe at home, especially at night while the porcupines are out eating.)

Bernice is a mature female Saint Bernard. While she should weigh in at about one hundred thirty pounds, she now weighs only ninety-five. It doesn't appear to be due to lack of appetite, either, and she has eaten very well since moving in here.

This dog makes me smile. On day one, she did only what was asked -went outside on a lead to do what needed to be done, and then slept soundly on the floor. On day two, she wagged her tail a couple of times when I spoke in a high pitched, happy tone to her and later that day, actually came to me for patting. She stopped ducking her head when I reached out to pat her on day three, and seemed to welcome the contact. She actually went for a walk with us, but stayed closely at my side. That night she slept on the biggest dog bed in my room. I heard her sigh contentedly several times during the night and smiled when she did a huge stretch this morning before she went out to the pen.

Her behaviour has been exemplary, even in light of Dreyfus' infatuation with her. She's slightly taller than that big guy, and, in proper condition, should outweigh him by about thirty-five pounds. I've never seen him to be so enamoured with another dog. I guess he likes the Amazons. I'm kind of enjoying the reprieve. Without Dreyfus taking every step I take, I'm less likely to go head over heels if I turn suddenly. Bernice is becoming less tolerant of his constant attentions though, and I expect she will address the situation soon. I've seen the warning signs, even if Dreyf hasn't. That Bernice is a saint to tolerate him for this long.

Anyway, I was heartened and flattered today when Bernice walked confidently up to me and laid her massive head in my lap, looking for attention. My welcoming smile was interrupted by a sudden yelp from me as I unquestionably identified a large quill that had been missed and was projecting from her lower jaw. Upon removing it from my leg, I regretted my noisy and profound reaction. I think that with intensive therapy, she will learn to trust me again soon. I don't suppose that she has had much experience with people shrieking and leaping to their feet when she greets them. With the offending quill gone, she has had a few pats and is starting to forget my strange behaviour. I, however, am now encouraging her to place her head on the arm of my chair so that I can dole out the neck massages and the ear rubs in comfort, and without frightening her further. Funny how one pointed object can ruin an otherwise well-planned session designed to promote trust and a feeling of well being.

In a well-deserved twist of fate, Hogan, is now the object of his own shenanigans as Bernice has started to make a game of herding him when they are running. I find it hard to summon up much pity for him when he finds his entire hind leg engulfed in Bernice's huge jaws. Jerry and Miles, the usual recipients of Hogan's compulsive herding behaviour, are enjoying a reprieve and I swear that I saw them both grinning the last time Hogan yelped. Hogan also seems to have acquired a random smattering of what appears to be huge strings of saliva over his entire back, causing him to step up his usual grooming routine (which is sparse at best.) Oh, well! What goes around...

My greatest wish for Bernice, now, is that after she is spayed, she will find a home that will understand and appreciate what a nice, sweet dog she is and that will treat her with the respect and love that she deserves. That's all DunRoamin' wants for all the little guys, or big gals, out there.

BOGART

Call me crazy, but we have yet another unadoptable dog at our home. He's had a hard life and was to be put down (ie: killed) because "he is not adoptable." Yes, he's old (many of us are). He smells, (he did, but a bath took care of that) and he has fleas (they are gone now) – so that leaves "old." Hmmm! Someone should have said that "old" is not adoptable before I looked at that "Charlton Heston" face and watched the greying eyebrows alternately raise and lower quizzically as he searched my face for some redeeming quality. Someone should have told me that his old body would leak a few drops of urine as he thrust himself into a standing position. Would that have been the deal breaker?

If I had known that this old dog, who would rest his craggy head on my lap and gaze trustingly into my eyes, was not adoptable, would I have brought him home and watched him decide to trust me and try to settle into my routine?

Until Each One Has a Home

If he is not adoptable, why are my dogs accepting him without question? Why am I sitting here grinning and watching him glory in the feel of the soft bed he now sleeps on, the bed that replaces whatever resting place that he could find in his previous life. Why do I smile as he stretches and moans in comfort at the softness and the warmth of his new bed? What makes me grin when he is fed supper, already having eaten breakfast that very same day? Why would I feel so content watching the worry of moving into a new house fade, replaced by a cautiously optimistic expectation of "good things" happening in this home? Why do I laugh out loud as I watch the interactions between this old fellow and his new roommates and see their instant acceptance of him? Why did I enjoy that last business trip of the day before we went to bed? How did I endure those grateful, gentle kisses this morning and how will I stand to see those soft gentle eyes following my movements with sheer relief and the beginnings of loyal friendship?

Of most concern regarding this unadoptable dog is how will I be worthy of this loyalty and devotion? I do know this without reservation – it took this unadoptable old dog a long time to get this sweet – and I'm not going to waste it! It is time that I entered into a mature relationship! And I've found just the guy!

ANNIE

This summer has been so nice for me. I have reconnected with my first best friend after about thirty years of living on different sides of the country. We have always had similar interests, which I find have continued over the long distance - except for one. I am an animal person and my friend does not feel comfortable around them. Although I know she has never wished them ill, she just prefers to avoid close contact. I get that! In fact, I remember one of the last times we went visiting friends, before she moved out west. A little boy had been given yet another pup and the family felt that they had no choice but to "dispose" of it. I remember impulsively saying that we would take it, and as we drove home, my friend holding the tiny thing at arm's length as if it was a bomb that would explode any minute. Then another thought struck her and she put the pup's tiny rear in a brown paper sandwich bag in case it "peed" on her. I remember thinking, "Those bags aren't waterproof!"

So, you can imagine my surprise when I dropped in at her house and she started to tell me, "Annie is a hero! She's a hero, you know!" I thought, "*The only Annie that I know in this family is a dog!*" As she progressed with the story, I realized that we were talking about Annie, the kindest, gentlest old Lab that I think I have ever met. I thought, "*Well, if anyone can adjust someone's discomfort around dogs, it would be Annie, with her total love and goodness.*" She'd worked her magic even before she became a hero, though. Slowly, insidiously, a bit at a time, she'd won her place in my friend's heart. Then, to be a hero, on top of that! Well, Annie has it made now: best treats, best dog sitter, best of everything, which she has certainly earned!

Oh, the hero thing! Yes, well, they had put some rhubarb on the stove to stew and were enjoying the sun on the deck and talking. After some time, Annie started pawing at the door. My friend thought that she was getting a hint that it was time to feed her but continued her conversation. Again, Annie pawed at the door, with no results. She continued her pawing, becoming more and more agitated until my friend decided to get her the food she wanted. On opening the door, she was met with black smoke from the rhubarb which was boiling over and burning on the stove. It could have been a much different result if not for the persistence of the old lab who is always watching out for her family.

That's the thing about Annie - she's smart, she's loving, she's everybody's friend - but family comes first! She would not rest until she got her message through to my friend - both messages: "Dogs are good!" and "You're gonna burn the house down!"

RIP BOGART

Well, bad news. The mature relationship that I had such great hopes for has fallen through - not through anyone's fault, certainly not Bogart's. You would be very hard pressed to find a guy of his calibre anywhere in this world. We had a great relationship! He became my boy. We had a wonderful, if short time together.

As often happens with these fragile old ones, his mind was willing but his heart was weak – his physical heart, I mean. His other heart was as big as Cincinnati and as pure and loving as any could be. We hoped that his lethargy that last day was due to tiredness. After all, our house is not the most restful place, with all the young dogs around. Certainly they did not purposely stress him – every dog accepted and liked him immediately. I think that it was his time and he was ready.

I'm glad that we got to spend his last few days with him, that he enjoyed warmth, comfort, turkey, cheese, pats, love,

Beggin' Strips, short walks in the yard, companionship and two square meals a day and water at his side. We worried that he wouldn't stay long, he was so old and in such poor condition. We rushed to add what goodness we could to his last few days. I think that his old body just gave out, but I think that he was happy, though, as he lay on his soft bed, with his head on my knee and fell asleep for the last time. I think he knew that we had tried to make his life better. I think he knew many more things than we gave him credit for. Wisdom shone from his old eyes . . .

I found this excerpt, written by an unknown author, which I think is super. This is for Bogie – rest in peace, my man.

> *"It came to me that every time I lose a dog, they take a piece of my heart with them, and every new dog that comes into my life gifts me with a piece of their heart. If I live long enough, all the components of my heart will be dog – and I will be as generous and loving as they are."*

MANLEY

Call me fickle, but I have to tell you about my newest favourite dog, Manley. He was removed from terrible living conditions by a strong DunRoamin' supporter who deals in rental properties. He's a six- or seven-month old pup, probably a Great Dane mix, black and tan with a little white and feet the size of dinner plates. He was given into her care as the owner "didn't want to be evicted because of the dog." He had it all wrong - he was going to be evicted because of his lack of care and cleanliness for the dog and its very confined living area.

Manley has fit in well here, and I find it hard to remember that he is a very inexperienced puppy. He's bigger than everyone here except Dreyfus (well, and me). His first trip to run in the field almost brought tears to my eyes. His gait was so loose that he fell several times while trying to run. Still, he had that happy "Look at me!" expression on his face and was happily exhausted when he climbed into my lap for a hug that night.

A week's worth of exercise has tightened his muscles and his gait is much stronger now - and faster! Again, Hogan is getting a taste of his own medicine. Now Manley can catch him occasionally and latches on to Hogan's tail. I hope the neighbours haven't heard the language Hogan is using lately.

This is the first time that I have fostered a pup who can grab the spiders from my hanging spider plant without climbing on a chair first. He is tall enough to get his own food from the counter – although I resent his attempts to do so. "Four on the floor!" I constantly tell him.

He's starting to be able to concentrate better now, too. Previously, he was so overstimulated by all the activity that he couldn't hear me ask him to do things. With persistence and large treat offerings, the little "Man" can now sit, lie down and go to bed on command. Oh, and he's very sure what "NO!" means. I needed new shoes anyway.

With help, we will find this great pup the home he needs, and help him to catch up on his development and training so that he can become the great friend that he was intended to be. I always feel so sad when we need to rehabilitate pups, no matter what the size. Still, Manley is just happy, now, to be clean, to have stimulation, to be able to run and play and to have a good hug now and then. He's also quite proud of his accomplishments in his understanding of language – the more he knows, the more treats he gets. I'm having a hard time to keep that kid's stomach full!

1-LEAN

Well, surprisingly, I have a new favourite cat! I don't take this admission lightly, but this little stray has inspired my admiration, as others have, with her strong will to live, her strength under adversity and her trust and acceptance of us (her proud caretakers and ardent admirers.)

This little survivor was driven to us from Debec where a young man noted her injuries and having never seen her before, took his morning to find help for her. (Thank you!)

When he arrived with the little cat, leaving a substantial donation to assist with her medical care, he was clearly upset at the damage done to her (as were we) but he had started her on the road to recovery by finding the help she needed.

This little calico tabby with the crossed eyes that goes with royal blood in her veins (Siamese) was very dehydrated, emaciated and had a high fever. Two inches of bone in one hind leg was exposed and covered with dirt. Still, she trustingly allowed us to examine her and treat her to stabilize her condition. In such terrible medical condition, this tough little cat, less than a year old, allowed us to care for her and then she used every bit of our assistance to become strong enough to make the necessary leg amputation feasible. That behind her, she has put her mind to recovering and becoming healthy again. Then, the second blow! The little fighter, now called I-Lean, has feline leukemia, a virus which is not treatable, and which is transmissible to other cats. This means that when she is healthy, she cannot live with other cats, unless they, too, carry this virus, so as not to spread it to others. This severely limits her possibilities for a home.

This makes me incredibly sad! But, like I-Lean, who hasn't given up, we won't either. We know that there is a home out there for such an amazing little cat whose short life has been so hard – and we won't stop until we find it.

Meanwhile, we'll keep her comfortable and happy. That's easy. She just needs her favourite food and plenty of chin rubs and petting. Oh, and I have to carry her around the clinic for a half hour every day, letting her look at the other patients and holding her up to look out the window so she can see the cows. I don't mind, I get well rewarded with purrs and kneading front feet. She is so cute. I don't mind that she leans –it's because of the lost leg.

Then I fix her a nice soft nest, put the bed warmer in and tuck my little friend into her little bed. Goodnight, I-Lean!

SPAY AND NEUTER

With the exception of kitten season, when those poor little struggling waifs come to us by the boxful, winter is the most terrible time for abandoned or discarded pets. Winter is the time when we see what our pets are really made of. At DunRoamin' and the Florenceville Vet Clinic (where the emergency care and treatment is initiated and the warming procedure of these half-frozen pets begins), we are steeling ourselves for the terrible things that we know will be coming in this winter. We know what will be coming because we have seen it year after year, the same awful injuries, the frozen body parts, the emaciated little bodies and the fear, exhaustion and pain in those innocent eyes.

We also are privileged to witness the strength, determination and will to survive in these little dogs and cats and the thankful acceptance of our warmth and assistance. That's why you see our volunteers and supporters eagerly fund-raising and working so hard to prepare. They have all seen, held or cried over the rescued pets who struggled under such adversity to survive on their own.

Their lives are every bit as important to them as ours are to us. And they overcome their hardships with such dignity, such grace and such appreciation for the assistance that they receive, that many humans could take a lesson from them. They are out there because of us, because we didn't spay or neuter or because we didn't care enough to care for them properly.

Please tell anyone who has not had their cats spayed or neutered that there are many assistance programs out there now to help with costs. DunRoamin' and the local shelter have sought and received a grant that helps to cover costs of cat spays and neuters for low income families. This is one way that we can help to decrease the overpopulation problem. We need people to take advantage of this grant or it will not be available to us in the future.

Remember that starting at five months of age, your female cat can have three litters per year, which can potentially work out to about eighteen babies every year. What would you do if you had eighteen babies every year? I know what I'd do: I'd book myself for a spay so quick that it would make your head spin!

So, while it seems that we spend a lot of time fundraising, that we're always out there with another fundraiser in the works, please know that because of your support the suffering and desperation of many little four-legged folk is ended and replaced with love, warmth and caring. Thank you for your efforts to support our pets in need.

CLAWED?

There are upsetting situations that we often see, many where the dog or pup seems to be the most intelligent member of the family. This, in itself, can mark the dog as a "bad" dog, right from puppyhood.

It started with a call from a woman who said that her last dog had had a parvovirus infection and that I had helped to save her dog even though she had no money at the time. She had since given that dog away and gotten a new pup several weeks ago. Now he had the same symptoms as the previous one. Now, I know myself well enough to know that, if I treated her pup at little cost to her, several things are true. First: She did not escape the lecture. You know, the one that explains how easily she could have avoided this illness by vaccinating the previous pup, how it is transmitted and all the work that she would have to do to abolish the virus in that pup's environment as well as the threat that this disease was to any other unvaccinated dog contact and that early vaccinations of any pup is much cheaper than treatment of the disease. Second: She was made well aware of the costs to me, the physical discomfort that the dog suffered and that she paid me at least the cost of vaccinations in payment for the drugs used to treat the dog. Third: She probably got a repeat of both above messages at the dogs discharge and was told that now that she knew about parvo, she could prevent it by vaccinating her animals and she could advise her friends and neighbours to do the same, and save many dogs from suffering the same fate.

So, I said to her, "Did I tell you about how parvo is passed and how important it is to have these little guys vaccinated?" "Yes," she replied, and I heard her take a large drag from her cigarette, "I was going to get it done!"" But you've had him for 6 weeks", I squealed. "I know, but I've been busy and he bites the kids" "What is it that you need from me?' I asked, as if I didn't already know. "I wondered if you would help me again," she said, "I don't have any money, right now."

I asked her to bring the pup to the clinic so that I could make a diagnosis before our discussion went any further. She was to pay for the parvo test and then we would resume our talk. Miffed that she had to pay for the test this time, when I hadn't charged her last time, she none the less agreed to bring the pup to me, because" she really loved this pup with all her heart!"

She arrived at the clinic with a very dehydrated, and feverish Shar pei/Mastiff mix pup, who, even in his lethargic state, was attempting to bite her if she moved him in the wrong way. I refused to treat the pup for its parvovirus infection at no charge but did offer to accept the pup under DunRoamin' and treat him, adjust his attitude and find him a new home. I felt this was very necessary since the little guy was leaving teeth prints and scratches on her hands even though she asked him not to since" Mommy loves you and it hurts her feelings when you bite Mommy!" Meanwhile, her children had made a thorough exploration of the clinic, investigating all the areas marked Staff Only, without their mother even noticing they were gone. (Nervous staff members had removed them from the most dangerous spots and were keeping them safe – not a glance their way from the mother.)

After much discussion, the owner decided to leave the biting, vomiting pup with me for treatment, refused to pay for his Parvo test, signed a surrender form (since no one she knew would lend her any money) and left the clinic. I turned out to be the bad guy in that situation.

We immediately got to work, starting IVs, administering antibiotics and analgesics and tried to settle the little guy and help him to manage his disease. Apparently he had never been taught that very important lesson involving a designation of who was in charge and who it was appropriate to bite.

As we were about to move him to his kennel, I had picked up the nasty little pup and heard Shannon say" Did you get clawed?" Unaware of the blood running down my forearm, and trying to think of an appropriate name for the little guy, I thought *"I'm not crazy about calling him Claude!"* but nevertheless, didn't argue with her choice of names. As we finished settling him into his kennel, Shannon indicated my arm and said "You did get clawed!" Laughing, I replied that I had thought that she was giving him that name. Given his behaviour, and lack of manners, we both agreed. "I did get clawed, he was getting called Claude but we were spelling his name C-l-o-d!

With proper treatment and support Clod was no time in recovering from his infection, still had a propensity to bite and was to be sent to my house for "Rehab". I was not very experienced in biting pups, but I did have my opinions on spoiled children who hit their parents and call them names. I knew what I would do if they were mine. Still, I had decided to research this puppy behaviour before trying to fine-tune the pup. As it turned out, I didn't have to do anything.

When the Clod arrived at my house, my dogs surprised me. I expected them to greet him, perhaps show him that they would not tolerate any shenanigans, and then either ignore him or start to play. I had watched these dogs greet rescued puppies many times.

To my surprise, all six of my dogs took turns walking up to that pup and putting him down on the floor. Only when he submitted, would they walk away. This went on interminably, until I started to think that it bordered on abuse. I have always trusted the dogs, saying that they knew more about dog behaviour than I did, and tried not to interfere. I could see that they weren't hurting him, but still, they would not allow him to regain his feet for more than a minute. At last, they let him stand, and I noticed some deferential looks from Clod. They continued their "tough love" for the rest of the day, until I realized that he was acting more like a normal pup, submissive to the adults, respectful of their glares and responsive to canine protocol.

Amazingly, I did not have to address the biting issue, except as a normal pup (be careful, don't bite too hard with those sharp teeth). I believe that my dogs rehabilitated that pup in their own way, with their own system. He became a sweet, squirmy little pup, as he was meant to be.

Clod, now grown and healthy, lives with a friend of the clinic and has never shown any abnormal aggression towards people or other dogs. Although he has a somewhat dominant attitude, he is a well-loved solid family member. It is a "lead or be lead" world. I think Clod led when he thought that he had to but was happy to shed the mantel of responsibility when an appropriate leader came along.

Diary of an Unchained Dog

Day 1:

This morning they took me off my chain and a stranger put me in his car. What will happen now? The stranger drove for a long time, then he gave my leash to someone else. I didn't know her either. What will happen? She is showing all her teeth at me! I'm scared! She put me in her car and drove me to another place. It looks like...I think...No-o-o-o-o! I've never been in the house before! She's taking me right in! I'm scared! I'm right inside the house!

There are other dogs inside the house. I don't see any chains. Those dogs go wherever they want. Wow! She took off my leash and she is letting me go! She's letting me explore and sniff anywhere I want. She's not even holding me back. I feel weird!

No, wait! She's putting me outside - there's no chain. She's just calling to me to come out – she's letting me go. Oh, the area has a big fence around it. It's hard to walk with nothing pulling on my neck. I feel...light and free. I guess I'll just follow the other dogs. Smells like they all pee here. OK, me too. They act like this is nothing special, like this is normal.

It's getting dark out. I hate the dark! Wait - we're all going in where the light is. I always wanted that so bad! I wonder when she will chain me. What does "Go to bed" mean? The others are lying on those soft things. Is that empty one for me? Should I lie down there? She's getting on her soft thing, too. Hers is very big. It's dark, but I am not alone. I hate being alone. I'm so tired.

Day 2:

I was in the house all through the dark and into the light and I was not alone. She says I am a "Good boy" and I am "Barack". It is not what she calls the others. She says a different thing for each one. We all go outside again and then get food. When does the chain come? She does such weird stuff. There is a place where water rains down but it's not a storm. I hate storms. You shouldn't drink from the big white water bowl there. That's OK. I know where the other one is.

Now we are going for what is called a walk. Is that a chain? There is no chain yet and we are all going right out through the pen into a big field. That must be where the chains are. The other dogs are barking and running. I'll try too. Ouch! What is a "face plant"? I'll try again and again until I can do what the others do. I'll enjoy it while I can. I feel so free - but I don't want to loose sight of her. It's like she is helping me or something. There, I didn't fall that time. One of the others has something called a "ball" but he won't let me have it.

Day 3:

This is awesome! I don't think she has a chain. She takes me to run and play and never chains me. I'm not alone either! So much stuff happens that my head is spinning. There are TVs and dishwashers and treat drawers that I didn't know existed. I love not being on a chain. I'm so tired. I love that, too.

Days 4-10:

I love everyone and everything! I almost caught the other dog! No more face plants! I love the bed. I love to sit. I can lie down. I love treats. I love her. She says that she will find a great home for me. She says I will be a family member in a big family and I will be happy with them. She says they don't have any chains. She says I will be a house dog, just like here. She says I will love it there and that now I will have a good life. I trust her now. I'd like to stay here but she says that if I stay she will not be able to help more chained dogs. I do trust her and I know how much chained dogs need help.

Day 11:

I met her-and him! I guess there are more in the family, too. They will all be mine. She has gotten me a whole family! I follow the new one around and rest my head on her feet when she sits down. I really like her. They will take me to their island in the sea. She says she needs me –I need her too. I have a big heart and can handle a lot of love. I will be their best friend- and they will all be mine.

No chains. No living outside. No loneliness. I don't mind the dark if I'm with them. I'm a housedog now. Thank you! Thank you! Thank you!

GREAT SCOT

One very disturbing condition that we see all too frequently is that in which an outdoor dog suffers from an embedded collar. This situation has many upsetting implications. They include the fact that the collar was placed on the dog when he was much smaller and he has effectively grown over the collar. This means that no one has noted the condition or placement of the collar for a very long time, that the strong odor of infection has been missed or ignored, that the dog is not in close proximity to attentive people and that he has remained on his chain for extended periods of time with no relief. More disturbing, is the knowledge that the collar or chain has been a constant source of pain and irritation for months. Try putting an elastic band tightly on your arm and leaving it in place for a week- this will not begin to approximate the discomfort suffered by these dogs. To fully understand, you would have to wait until the elastic had embedded itself into the skin and left a wound two or three centimeters wide and one to two centimeters deep, become severely infected, and the oozing of the infected material had caused a skin infection below the wound and extending for eight to ten centimeters on the surface.

These were the circumstances that had prevailed when I met Scotlund. Named for the leader of the Animal Rescue Corp, a group that works continuously to rescue groups of animals from unacceptable conditions, the dog's appearance might stop some attempts at friendship. At one hundred and ten pounds the shepherd/St. Bernard cross was an imposing animal, with his muscular body and his huge, broad head, accentuated by the blood and secretions surrounding his entire neck and his scruffy coat. His behaviour revealed that he was not used to being in a house, or a car. He had difficulty walking on smooth floors and frequently slipped and lost his footing if moving too rapidly. Worse, he ducked when a hand reached for him and was wary of shovels, brooms, sticks and other potential assault weapons.

But look into his light brown eyes and you are lost in a huge pool of unconditional love and unending goodness. Despite the unspeakable conditions of his life and the ever-present pain encircling his entire neck, this dog loves people. If you are not sold by the love in his eyes, his demeanor will convince you in no time. I can only recall one other dog that was greeted by my dogs with the warmth that Scotty received. (That was a very weak female who had been shot in the head and in the back and left to die in the woods.) My guys, rather than greeting him with the aggressive postures that they had used on the golden female pup, just two weeks prior, walked slowly towards the massive dog and greeted him with concern. (Did you hurt your neck? Are you OK?) Their greeting was returned in a very gentlemanly fashion, introductions were completed and the bachelor herd settled down for a nap. (There were no sports on the TV at the time.)

That huge fellow was a delight, learning to greet people with confidence and oozing goodness and stability. I was fortunate to be there when Scotty met his new family. To watch him walk beside his new friend, leash loose, and looking down into the little boy's eyes made my throat tighten and I couldn't swallow. Despite having just met them, Scotty seemed to know that they were his family, and he waited while the children were safely in their car seats before climbing in the van, as if he had been doing it all his life.

His progress reports are glowing and I am confident now, that this is a dog that I will never need to worry about again. He has a wonderful family to do that for him, finally.

Meet DunRoamin's Barack

Well, you know that I love new experiences- but I was just sideswiped by a dog! Pardon me for making it such a big deal, but I was sure they all came with anti-lock friction brakes or at least pumping brakes. I don't think this guy even knows that he has a brake pedal.

Not that he's ever had much of a chance to use it. This is probably the first time that he's revved his engine to "Race" in a very long time. Still, you'd think he would watch where he's going! Especially at that speed!

I guess I can forgive him for his exuberance since this is his first week off the chain and he's still less than a year— a puppy still. But, I was right there, hadn't moved and I'm amazed that he didn't see me, or kill me. Now I know how bowling pins must feel. Oh, I'm sure the bruises will fade in time.

I call him Barack. Whether he was born in the US or not, he may have relatives there. In the week that I have known him, I have concluded that this dog is, indeed, a Democrat. He is not about to use all his resources in a military effort. He is not pushing for a fight, preferring to use diplomacy whenever possible. He believes in equality and social justice. He does not believe in chains.

Like his namesake, Barack is quite capable of using humour and fun to defuse situations and to gain followers. He has a certain likable, self-deprecating way about him, despite the strength and power he wields. (He's eighty pounds of muscle and energy)

Also, like his namesake, he believes that we must fight the good fight to make this world a better place for man and beast. Like the other Barack, he believes that "Change will not come if we wait for some other person or some other time. We are the ones we have been waiting for. We are the change that we seek."

Unlike his namesake, though, he is not looking for a position that is short term or that is politically decided. The position to which he aspires is one that is long-term and lifelong. He wants to devote his entire life to his mission. He wants his position, his home, to be forever!

THE SAINT BERNARD DOG BLOG

Day 1

Call me crazy (many have), but I was down to only four dogs — all my own— and it was just too easy. So- now I have a little husky friend staying with me and, today, a second foster dog. I may outweigh this new guy by a pound or two and have nowhere near the jowls and chins that this dog has, thank goodness! However, I do have more determination and resolve than he does and I am a much bigger bitch than he has seen since he left his mother.

I am no saint – as many would agree, but this guy is –a saint, I mean, a Saint Bernard, with little to no training and what seems to be a horrible and abusive history. He's only two and he eats more than the combined feedings of my other five dogs. I find that a towel is my best friend today. Oh, his name is Bach. More later.

Day 12

Things are not going according to plan with my new friend, Bach. I am falling for the big guy, and find him to be more endearing as each day passes. Big problem –I already have five dogs. He is behaving so well, with no aggression towards the other dogs, even though the evil Sioux, the ancient Anatolian shepherd, attacks him at every opportunity. Now he simply side-steps her attack, watches her fall and seems to say" Missed me!"

Bach did make a scene at work the other day when someone left the door to the waiting room opened. Excitement at meeting a new friend, then further excitement at realizing the new friend's cat was not in a friendly mood, necessitated staff removing Bach and incarcerating him in a kennel. That hurt his feelings and he did voice his displeasure, but quickly forgave everyone when he was released.

He went on his first free walk with the other dogs a few days ago. It was fun! I think Bach loves me back –he returns to me, when called, faster than any of the other dogs. Well, they have to get back to their feet after being plowed down by him, but still…

He is actually a gentle, if foolish, giant. He now trusts that I am not going to hit him, so no more ducking from hands, and no hiding from brooms or shovels.

Bach needs that special owner who can stand drool and adoration. Those are his requirements. Oh, and they need to be able to love him and to treat him with the love and respect that this little boy needs. I promised him that I would find him a good home.

Day 18

More about the foster dog, Bach. He is big! His head rests on my chest and completely covers me. I move away in discomfort as my shirt is covered with drool. It is on my floors (and is very slippery), my walls, my furniture and my clothes. I was pleased to discover a six-inch strand of dried crusty drool on the back of my coat sleeve while paying for groceries this afternoon.

I have just decided to wear a shower curtain for the foreseeable future while I get him trained, neutered and ready for a new home.

Interestingly, I found an inch of clear slime in the dogs' large water bowl today when I was cleaning it. That's a first and very, very gross. Also found lots of slime in his food bowl, and in the five-foot radius of that bowl when I cleaned up tonight.

He's a sweetheart in the temperament department and has already learned the tip off edge that is in my voice when I am getting annoyed. He waits till the very last minute before complying, but does so with such grace and good humour that he makes me smile.

Having Bach here has certainly benefited my upper body strength as he uses his huge body as a plow to get where he wants to be. I am hoping that this extra workout doesn't make me bulk up with all the weight that I am working against.

Thankfully he is beginning to see things my way, is learning to respect boundaries and allows me to take the lead most of the time.

Jerry, the shepherd, just wants me to take Bach to the dump. Jerry is totally fastidious about his appearance and cannot stand any dirt on his coat. The big guy thinks it is funny to pull Jerry around by his back leg and the amount of resulting drool on his coat is driving Jerry insane. Bach doesn't notice drool, I think, but Jerry and I do so we keep towels with us at all times.

I can't believe what a mellow, tolerant dog this guy is and how he is so funny and teases the other dogs like some monstrous puppy, yapping at them and getting on their nerves while spittle and drool flies about the house. Maybe I can pay someone to come in daily to wash the walls –but, then, what would be the point?

Day 22

Interesting factoid: I have discovered that errant strands of dog saliva (also known as drool or goobers) when missed during the hourly toweling of the furniture and walls, will, given time, collect and adhere to large amounts of dog hair that may be floating around the room. After the passage of sufficient amounts of time during which the saliva dries completely, said goober can then be easily vacuumed up, along with the adhesed dog hair, leaving no visible residue on furniture, walls or floors.

So-you can see my quandary. Hourly toweling or daily vacuuming.

Day 35

It seems that many have been bothered by the fact that I have given my foster dog, Bach, the Saint Bernard, such a discordant name. Well, let me explain. It seemed very obvious to me, on his arrival, that this dog was no Beethoven, but was noteworthy himself. He, too, seemed like one of the great composers, and, although he has no movie experience, he is, in fact, a virtuoso in his own right. His appearance here, and his discordant, staccato voice has given new meaning to the words *vocal quality*. When asked to modulate his sound he has vented in anger, as a true artist.

Oh, did I say composer? I meant composter! With his style and form, he has fertilized the dog yard with such a smooth distribution, that it alone has been instrumental in the upsurge of back pain that is sweeping my body- the result of the content that must be stooped to scoop.

That dog has orchestrated some of the most foul situations that this house has ever seen. Still, in concert with the other dogs he has modulated his sound and behaviour and is blending in much more smoothly.

On other levels this arrangement with the composter, Bach, has become a fine symphony, which flows into a harmonious melody of love and respect with overtones of comfort and relief. It could, in fact, be called a *rhapsody of home* for

Bach. He is learning how to play and enjoy the freedom to be the composter extraordinaire that he aspires to be, a talent that is at his very center. How much better could it get?

Day 50

What a dog! This great big, drooly, awkward guy, who epitomizes the word Blockhead, has learned his obedience and happily responds to commands with an "I know this one" attitude! He's so cute and personable, he still makes me laugh. He has progressed so far – amazingly. I can't help but wonder who this dog would have been if he had had a decent start in life, with a caring owner who socialized and taught this dog, rather than beating him with a shovel.

Day 90

Sadly, I must now report that the Saint Bernard, Bach, is no longer with us. He had to go home where he will always be loved and never have to face harm and abuse again.

After three months with me, during which he became socialized, obedience trained, and was taught to live loose with the other dogs (and was neutered), he had to go. I was so proud of his accomplishments! A voice in my head kept saying "Adopt him", but another voice, the voice of reason said" You have four big dogs and another foster, that's all you can handle now!" I hate that voice.

His personality was becoming more open and playful. He greeted me with wagging tail and drool splattering on my feet, so happy to see me, after our five minute separations. He learned to play ball, to sit for a treat, and just exactly how to look at me to get the hug that he wanted. He had overcome so much.

The other morning, as I was letting all six dogs outside, I grabbed him by his collar, as I did every morning, to prevent him from knocking my old dog down as they passed through the door. Whether the manner in which I grabbed his collar brought back memories of the abuse that he had suffered, prompting a PTSD-like flashback, or whether he had a seizure like episode, I will never know. In seconds, whatever the cause, I had multiple and deep bite wounds to my face, head and arms. As I managed to stand, I said "Bach, Sit!" and he responded immediately. I like to think that he had a confused expression on his face but that may be just my shock. The emergency room doctors informed me that a smaller person or child would have surely been killed and that my own injuries had barely missed vital functions.

Attempts to place this big guy in a Giant Breed Rescue with behaviourists to help him to cope with his past were unsuccessful. (We had contacted many when we first got him.) Due to the large numbers of these popular giant breeds being produced now, often by incompetent, uneducated breeders, giant breed rescues are overflowing. This and the attack left me with no options but to euthanize this beautiful dog, for safety reasons. His size and the severity of his bites left us with no alternatives.

As I was being attended to in the emergency room, my friends and colleagues, Shannon and Lynn, guided the big guy on his way to Rainbow Bridge, where he will never face abuse again. I was told that, while waiting for his sedation to take effect, he ate two packages of hotdogs and a pound of cheese. That made me smile – he was such a food hound.

This poor, poor dog did not stand a chance in this world. The product of careless breeding, placed in an abusive home, not socialized or trained and then passed from home to home, with new owners planning to shoot him when he didn't measure up. If even half of the reports are accurate, Bach suffered from isolation, boredom, severe beatings (several reports said that a shovel was the tool of choice), lack of shelter, - a life of Hell at the hands of several owners.

How could that dog not have stability issues? How much therapy would a human survivor of such treatment require?

For Bach, and many others, I would like to make this point. Do you know who always pays for our treatment of and mistakes in managing and training our dogs?

The dog! The dog always pays. That huge dog, full of life and love, carelessly bred, carelessly placed, abused, neglected, unsocialized – Bach didn't stand a chance!

Well, RIP, Puppy. No more suffering for you! Go home! I hope to see you later.

That dog, that poor, poor Bach, paid with everything he had.

DunRoamin's Omen

It may be that Dr. Monteith and I have come up with a new treatment modality. At least it seems to have worked for us this time. A few more clinical trials should give us more information on its effectiveness.

I guess I should start at the beginning and tell you about one of the most loving and loved patients that we have seen in a long while. In dire straits, this black cat came to the back porch of a home in Perth Andover and, his rescuers, realizing he was in trouble, brought him to DunRoamin'. His body condition was poor, but his abdomen was distended. He had fleas and was allergic to them, causing a painful, itchy rash. His black coat was brittle and straw-like and had a reddish tint, suggesting chronic poor nutrition –and his left eye socket was empty and infected. Still he was happy to greet his new family, welcomed the availability of good food, and seemed to improve over the next weeks. He was cared for by

DunRoamin' volunteers and quickly became a favorite –partly due to his endearing habit of putting both front legs around the neck of anyone who picked him up and rubbing his face on their chin.

Even though he was subjected to uncomfortable treatments, such as flushing the debris from the empty eye area, and receiving medications that "tastes awful but it works", this little guy, now known as Omen, rejected the use of violence to defend himself. He might push a hand away, but never used teeth or claws. He became the unlikely darlin' of DunRoamin'.

So— it was with great anxiety that his caretakers reported to the vet clinic that Omen had stopped eating and was not responding to social interactions. He was moved to the hospital where his veterinarian determined that his blood was extremely low (almost too low to support life) and his abdomen was very distended. With several days of treatment, Omen continued to deteriorate, despite offerings of hugs, special foods and a commitment by the cat caretaker to adopt him if he would only live.

A few days before Christmas, Dr. Monteith and I stood in front of Omen's kennel to discuss his lack of response to treatment and to brainstorm regarding other treatment options. We came up with none. We did decide to give him a couple more days to see if he could respond to our medications and start eating on his own. We concluded our consultation by agreeing that if his blood had not improved within the next couple of days, or if he still refused to eat, we would not condone his suffering and agreed to euthanize him.

Galvanized, volunteers begged him to get better. Clinic staff home-cooked chicken and hamburger. On one visit to check on Omen's condition, I noted an entire smorgasbord of food available to him in his kennel – chicken, hamburger, salmon, cat milk, recovery cat food, and cheese. Not wanting to disappoint anyone, I guess, Omen ate! Then, when picked up for a congratulatory hug, Omen hugged back. His bloodwork that morning was improved. The clinic was in celebration status, as was DunRoamin'.

You know, that little fighter, not the most attractive of cats, even without the empty eye socket, had an entire cheering section rooting for him- all because of his lovely personality and his strength in fighting to survive. He may be a black cat—but he's certainly a good Omen!

Maybe we will discuss our plans to euthanize them in front of other critically ill cats, giving them forty-eight hours to improve. Was that the impetus? Time will tell. We all agree. We really don't care how or why he did it - just that he's still here with us. Still, if it works, we'll do it again.

Wiley

That poor little guy! Given to a stranger who took him to his home and let him loose. Attacked by the stranger's dog and chased off into the woods. Then afraid to return or to trust anyone –they were all strangers to him. And still less than one year old. He lived on the lam all winter, while an SPCA officer used most of her spare time trying to catch him- but he was too afraid, couldn't trust anyone. Neighbours made him beds with straw and put food out. Finally caught in a live trap, he was close to death. His tibia and fibula on his right hind leg were shattered beyond repair and he had a through and through gunshot wound in his thigh. His foot was easily three times normal size and the skin was sloughing. The leg was simply a bag of pus. We amputated to try to save his life.

Once recovered from his high fever and his infection, he showed us that he wanted to be friends, but wasn't sure who to trust - and, if he went outside on a leash, would he get back in?

During his hospitalization, he made many friends but it was evident that he wanted to be someone's dog, that he wanted to belong to someone. That is the way with German shepherds.

As his health improved, it became evident that he wanted to be more active and, when he was ready, I took him to my house. I have a fenced area just off my living room and plenty of other dogs for him to play with. No more boredom.

After two days in my home, he tentatively started to play with Jessie, a young Siberian husky foster dog. After five days, he would race outside into the pen, play for a few minutes, then race inside, landing in my lap for a hug, stay for a minute or two then, look at me as if to say "Well, gotta go" and race outside for more play. His eyes began to sparkle as if he was enjoying life again. Then he met her - the girl that he wanted to spend his life with. Swallowing the lump in my throat, I let him leave with her, knowing he was better off with her than competing for attention with seven other dogs.

Then I get the call. "Did you know Wiley is loose and won't let anyone catch him?" His new owner had made a rookie mistake in letting him off-lead too soon and he had become frightened and too afraid to come to anyone. I raced to the site and although I caught glimpses of him, I realized that he had reverted to his behaviour of the previous winter. His flight responses were again keeping him from being caught. After several hours and in complete darkness, I left, bereft and planning to return at first light.

My Border collie, Hogan, with me, I returned to the site at daybreak to learn that he had been seen nearby, just moments before. Hogan and I walked the treeline next to the river where he had last been seen. I talked quietly and gently, speaking his name frequently. "Wiley, puppy, come on, you know you can trust me. Come on, Wiley! Jeez, what in Heck is your problem? Not as if you haven't been sleeping with me for three weeks. Am I that easy to forget? "Suddenly, Hogan became very alert, looking into the trees. "*OK.*" I thought," *It's either Wiley or one of the bears that inhabit the treed river shore.*" Placing my trust in Hogan's body language (he didn't seem scared) I said "Go find Wiley" and watched him leap into the trees. Seconds later, I heard crackling branches and scuffing sounds that I interpreted as the two dogs greeting each other and then I smiled as Hogan trotted into view, followed closely by Wiley, who leaped into my arms. I guess he wasn't sure that it was really me until he got my scent from Hogan.

Back home, exhausted, I thought that I would assess his mental state after I had had a short nap. I can never sleep while an animal is missing, especially one with the terrible history that Wiley had.

Wiley, legs and body covered in dried mud, and burdocks in every part of his coat, climbed into bed with me, laying his head on my shoulder and emitting a long, exhausted sigh. "No, Wiley," I muttered, "You are covered with dirt and burrs and ...Whatever!". Unable to summon the energy to move him, I accepted his closeness and drifted off to sleep. Hours later I awakened to a gritty feeling, as if I was sleeping at the beach and opened my eyes to find the bed covered with dried mud and the front of my shirt covered with pieces of burdocks. As I slept, Wiley had started the process of cleaning himself up – pulling out the burdocks and spitting them on my shirt.

Some of My Foster Dogs

<u>Classie:</u>

I have, well, I guess you could say – a bone to pick, with my newest foster dog, Classie! She was removed from her life as a chained dog, with a rusted out car for shelter, found to be unfit as a pet after several hours in her new home, and then placed in the Classifieds in the local paper. She was unwanted because she was untrained and had a small skin issue. Thankfully, she was accepted by DunRoamin'.

This lovely, black and tan hound-like dog is so happy to be with people and dogs. She will make someone a great pet. Not to be a complainer or anything, but my problem right now is that, not only is she a bed hog (uninvited), but, I guess she gets cold, because I had to fight all last night for enough blankets to cover myself.

Tonight she gets her own blanket, only half of the bed – Hogan, Jerry and I need the other half, and a forceful, if whiny "No" when she kicks me for more room.

Apart from this one issue, I find her to be delightful—gentle, obedient, and happier as each day passes. She will make someone an excellent pet- maybe someone with a king-sized bed, or fewer dogs in the bed. Yes, that should work. I'll start looking.

Royce:

I think that my foster dog has passed his "Best Before" date. Little Royce, the Sheltie cross, was so good and so sweet for the first three weeks as a DunRoamin' dog. During that time we fixed his chronically broken hip and gave him time to heal. Now- well, NOW he is rotten.

Yesterday was an example of how this little guy has deteriorated. Poor Woody, my other foster, a Saint Bernard and something very strong and short haired cross, has been pushed beyond the limits of decency. Not only is Royce jumping on him each time he tries to sleep, but he has been using poor Woody as a soft bed, a chew toy, a herding victim, a Ninja target, and a stationary jungle gym.

If he's not sleeping on top of him, he is attacking him out of the blue, or hanging from various parts of Woody's anatomy. Woody has reached the limits of his tolerance for the spoiled little youngster, barking at me to get this "stinking pup" away from him. The loathsome little devil is only good for a few seconds before he returns to biting Woody's legs or ears.

Any fun is tainted by the persistence Royce shows in his torment of Woody. His truces are untrustworthy, with him sneaking up on his target from different directions.

It leaves a festering attitude of revenge in Woodrow's head and, I must admit to a smile of satisfaction when Woody bests the little trouble maker, and sits on him for extended periods.

In his defence, though, I think the foul behaviour and unmitigated gall of this pup is simply the result of a young dog, finally freed from the severe pain and suffering that has been his life since he was very young. Free of that severe pain, he has begun to enjoy life, and Woody. Woody wants to know if he is returnable.

Shogun

Another of my newest favorite foster dogs is an eighteen month old, unneutered Shar pei /Lab mix who has spent the last six months at a shelter. He was said to be both people and dog aggressive and felt to be unmanagable by the shelter staff. Due to multiple recent staff turnovers and the inexperience of staff, his reputation had become worse and worse until euthanasia was considered due to his behaviour and the lack of time to exercise and interact with him.

He was brought to the vet clinic for an assessment. His reputation had preceded him and the waiting area had been cleared of people and animals.

Having not yet met the dog, I had nontheless given him a name -Shogun, and was expecting a aggressive Asian military warlord. The animal who flew into the clinic at the end of that leash was a mix of a whirling dervish and a Tasmanian devil. He had two Border Collies worth of energy and, I was told, hadn't had a run in months. He had no idea what manners were and flung himself towards anything that caught his attention.

Lifting him down from the counter for the second time, I took his leash, blocked him from bolting into the OR and said: "No" as he lunged for the technician's lunch on a nearby table. He stopped dead, looked a me as if to say "Really?" then began to modify his behaviour slightly as he accepted my direction.

There was no aggression as I was deliberately rude to him and he easily submitted to my wishes. I removed objects from his mouth, towered over him and picked up his feet. OK, no people aggression. Then we introduced him to the long suffering, laid-back Husky mix, Lamar. Shogun was overly enthusiastic in checking Lamar out but showed no aggression and easily accepted Lamar's wish that he back off. Introductions to two other dogs revealed inexperience with dog manners but no aggression.

So- he's at my house. He is a forty pound bundle of untrained, inexperienced, overly enthusiastic, hyperactive, uninhibited, panting, quivering, jumping, constantly moving blur of inquisitiveness, tempered by good intentions -sort of the doggie equivalent of a perpetual motion machine crossed with Mr. Bean.

Some of my dogs even like him a little, although Miles, my thirteen year old Border collie mix and second in command, has had to speak to Shogun a few times. The pup has responded appropriately to Miles' reprimand and shows the respect that is required.

All he needs now is some manners training, lots of exercise and someone to love him. I think I can set that up. There is a wonderful place just this side of Fredericton called Paw and Order, which offers dog day care, training and exercise. The owner and staff are amazing with dogs and DunRoamin' is very fortunate to have their help in placing some of our rescue dogs. There he can get the supervised experience with other dogs that he needs, manners training and lots of loving attention. He can't help but thrive there and they have been very successful in finding just the right home for many of our dogs.

Disturbing thoughts keep repeating in my mind. How many decisions to put dogs down when they cause disturbances in a shelter setting, are made by trained people? How much exercise do some shelter dogs get? Who monitors the conditions and the outcomes for dogs held in shelters? Who has the right to kill a dog because that dog is not adapting to shelter life? When will their lives become worth something?

HALLE PLEAS FOR HELP

Dear Mr. Editor,

My name is Halle and I need your help. I have been looking for my family for two years now, as has my brother, Martin. We were abandoned on the Plymouth Road along with eleven other sick cats. Perhaps you remember our story - we are referred to as the Dirty Dozen. The eleven others have found their families, but we have not been able to find ours.

Our family might be one with children, a dog or perhaps other cats. They may have no children, may be an older couple or maybe a single person. We don't know because we have never met them. Although we have never seen them, we know they are out there. The volunteers who come to look after us are always looking out for them and constantly tell us "Maybe your family will come today, maybe they'll find out where you are and come to take you home!" We are three years old now and always try to look our best because they say that we never know when our family will walk in. We've been worried because we might not be as pretty as the other cats, since we both lost one eye because of how sick we were when we first came here. The volunteers say our family will love us because of how we have survived and because we waited so long for them. The volunteers say we are 'good cats'.

It's not our family's fault. They just don't know where to look. Maybe they have already been to DunRoamin' but didn't see me (I am a little shy), but Martin is very friendly and always looking for hugs. He says he will know his family when they hug him. Maybe they haven't been here, but everywhere they go, they peek around a corner, expecting to see me. Maybe they sit on their couch at night and look at the empty spot on their laps or beside them on the couch where I should be.

Maybe they do housework, talking away to me, then realize that I am not there to provide advice and support. Maybe they come home from a busy day at work and need the snuggles that I can provide and realize how much they miss me. I don't want to let them down. They need me!

So, please, Mr. Editor, if you happen to see my family, or hear about them in your newspaper, would you let them know that I am here and so is Martin. Tell them that I know that I will love them once we meet, and that I will be the best cat they have ever had. So will Martin, if they need two cats.

I just know they are out there, looking for me as much as I am looking for them. I know they are missing me and they need me!

Mildred A. Drost DVM

Still patiently waiting,

Halli (and Martin)

AFTERWORD:

The essays presented here in this book reflect attitudes, feelings and thoughts that resulted from the plight of the pets that have come to our rescue –DunRoamin' Stray and Rescue,Inc.

Attempts to lighten some of the content with 'dark humour' are done, not to lessen the impact of the appalling conditions of these animals, or to minimize the situations that these pets have survived but are a common coping mechanism used by many professionals who deal with disturbing situations. Other light articles are written to pay tribute to the animals themselves and to acknowledge the very important contributions that animals make to our quality of life.

Anyone involved in animal rescue, rehabilitation and rehoming anywhere in the world will recognize the situations, is familiar with the unfairness and the cruelty that many pets face and is familiar with the hope to influence others to respect, revere and appreciate all of the animals in our world.

The very common attitude that a dog is not allowed to bite, under any circumstances, is a good example of our attitude towards animals. When I hear some people talk about their dogs and how they have trained them using totally misguided beliefs and no understanding of the dog itself, I often think that it is not surprising that some dogs bite. Then I quickly realize that, what is actually amazing, given the few dogs who actually do bite, is that many, many more dogs don't bite us out of fear, frustration and confusion and due to our misunderstanding of our closest friends, their needs and their often difficult and unrewarding relationships with us. This speaks to the goodness of dogs –man's best friend. This extends to our relationship with all animals. It would be so easy for us to treat them better, to understand their needs and to allow them to have better lives. My greatest hope is that more of us will become our pet's best friend and become friends to all animals. It would be to the betterment of both man and animal.

As DunRoamin' volunteers cope with their load of needy animals, mostly cats and dogs, but with the occasional wild patient included –raccoons, squirrels, mink, crows, woodpeckers, mourning doves, foxes and coyotes, - all are tended to with equal care and concern, always with the animal's best interests in mind, I can almost hear them thinking "I made a difference for that one!" Now, we need to try to make a difference for all of them.